MEDICINAL POWER OF PLANTS
Best Solution to Health Problems

ADAMU DEDE MURZA

DEDICATION

This book is dedicated to my beloved parent Dede Ali Murza
and Amina Hassan

CONTENTS

ACKNOWLEDGMENTS

All praises be to God almighty for given me the opportunity to undertake this great task. I thank Him for enriching plants materials with cure for the diseases and illness prevailing on the surface of the earth, as well as bestowing man with the ability to find out for the benefit of all. I am also grateful to my teachers including Prof. D.B Dangora, Prof. A.K Adamu, Prof. F.K lawal and Prof. Muhammadu Abdullahi, to mention but few, who assisted me immensely in the course of my academic journey. I will not forget my HOS Mal. Iliya Nuhu for all the support rendered to me. I also thank my family members, friends and well-wishers.

INTRODUCTION

It has been estimated by the World Health Organisation that most of the developing countries use herbal medicine as the first line of treatment of disease. Almost 120 pharmaceutically produced drugs are derived from plant materials. The sell and consumption of plant-based medicine is increasing throughout the world. As a result, the WHO recognised programmes that aimed at integrating traditional medicines into their primary health care programmes. This recognition led to conference of 1978 organised by WHO in USSR, in which the member countries resolve initiate programmes of research in identifying, cultivating and conservation plants used in traditional medicine as well as ensuring quality control of drugs that are developed from plant remedies by using modern techniques and applying suitable standards and good manufacturing practices. In other to achieve this effort, Organization of African Unity (now African Union) and Governments declared the period 2000-2010 as the period of African Traditional Medicine. Later on, 2001 Abuja Declaration called on the Member States to give priority to research on traditional medicines used for the management of diseases such as HIV/AIDS, malaria, TB and other infectious diseases. The African Union Summit which took place in Maputo in 2003 endorsed the WHO proposal to institute the African Traditional Medicine Day in Member States on 31st August of every year as part of a strategy to promote traditional medicine in health systems. Africa has abundance of plants, many of which have medicinal values today. Important examples of medicinal plants which are commercially exploited are Rauwolfia vomitoria (majorly a tranquilizer and antihypertensive agent), reserpine (e.g Zingiber officinale) used for its carminative and anti-inflammatory properties, Catharanthus roseus, a source of the anti-tumour agents, vinblastine and vincristine and Phytolacca dodecandra, used as an effective molluscicide to control schistosomiasisone text here.

MEDICINAL PLANTS

1. Acacia nolitica

Botanical Name	Acacia nolitica
Common Name	Egyptian mimosa (English), Gonakier, Acacia du Nil (French)
Local Name	Burkina Faso: Moore- Peg-nenga,Bogonan, Fulfulde-Gaoudi;Gawdi
	Ghana: Akan – Odanwoma
	Mali: Bambara – Bagana, Malinke – Bagana, Dogons – Barin
	Nigeria: Hausa – Bagawura
	Niger: Hausa – Bagaroua, Djerma – Baani Senegal: Wolof – Gonaki, Serer – Nep Nep; Pular – Gaudi

Description	A spiny tree can grow up to 20 m high. Dark-brown to black bark, deeply fissured or cracked, with pinkish-grey slash, exuding a reddish resin; stems, olive green to brownish. Leaves alternate, bipinnate, blue-shaded, 4-10 cm long.
Habitat and Distribution	Northern savanna regions and its range extend from Mali to Sudan and Egypt.
Plant Part of Interest	Fruit
Chemical constituents	Tannins ([-]epigallocatechin galloyl esters), alkaloids, saponins, proteins (Kumaresan et al., 1984; Ramana et al., 2000; Sawe et al., 1998; Mlambo et al., 2008).
Ethnomedical Uses	Nilotica can be used in treatment of bronchitis, chest pains, colds, diarrhoea, dysentery, fever, haemorrhage, leprosy, eye disorders, pneumonia, sore throat syphilis oral candidiasis; fungal skin infections, malaria and toothache (Chhabra and Uiso, 1991; Watt 1962), syphilis (Kambizi and Afolayan 2001; Watt 1962)
Precaution for Use	May cause a reduction in body weight
Dosage and Dosage form	Decoction, concoction, ointment, poultice Decoction: 30 g of dried leaves in 900 ml of water, boil until

reduced to 600 ml, 1 teaspoon three times a day.

2. Adansonia digitata

Botanical Name	Adansonia digitata
Common Name	Egyptian mimosa (English), Gonakier, Acacia du Nil (French)
Local Name	Burkina Faso: Mooré-twèga, Dioula-Sira, Fulfuldé-bolbe;bouki. Ghana: Akan-Odadeē. Mali: Bambara-Zira, Manlinké-Sito, Dogon-Oro Niger: Hausa-Kouka, Djerma-Kogna. Nigeria: Yoruba-Ose. Senegal: Wolof-Gui, Gouïe; Serer-Bàk, Diola-Bu Bak, Hausa-Kuka Sierra leone: Fula-Sule, Kono-Sela, Madingo-Sida Togo: Moba-Tokala, Ewe-Adidotsi, Nawdem-Todi
Description	The plant has a characteristic of large tree of size 15-20 m long. It has a hard, spongy, thick and large trunk of about 20 m in diameter that usually spread out and contorted. The bark is greyish brown in colour and is normally smooth but can often be variously folded depending on the years of growth. Leaves are alternate, digitate with entire or denticulate margin, and composed of six to seven leaflets. The leaf shape is obovate or

	ovate, acuminate, acute, slightly pubescent on the surface. Flowers are large, white, solitary, pendulous (10-20 cm), with very long stalks up to 80 cm (Kerharo and Adam, 1974). Fruits are capsules and are called monkey bread, which are oblong, ovoid or rounded, woody and hairy of about 8-15 cm wide which is suspended at the end of a long stalk. The epicarp is greenish, at maturity and contains numerous black hard seeds in a white floury pulp.
Habitat and Distribution	The plant grows in the thorny woodlands of the African savannas, which has low altitudes with limited annual rainfall like the Sudano-Sahelian zone. It survives in hot, dry woodland on stoney, well drained soils, but adapts to any soil.
Plant Part of Interest	Leaf, fruit pulp
Chemical constituents	Contains vitamin A, B and C. it also contains minerals (calcium, phosphorus), mucilage, protein, cellulose, anthraquinones, saponins, sterols and triterpenes, amino acids (apart from cystine and tryptophan), organic acids (citric acid, tartaric acid, malic acid, stearic acid, linoleic acid, palmitic acid) (Gaiwe, 1989; Kerharo and Adam, 1974; Toury et al. 1957).

Ethnomedical Uses	A. digitata is used to treat worm infestations, diarrhoea and abdominal pain (Diehl et al., 2004). Decoction of the root or stem bark is used as a disinfectant for chronic wounds. Juice from fresh stem bark is applied to small inflammated boils, whilst a powder mixed with Lannea microcarpa seed oil is applied to large boils (Inngjerdingen et al., 2004). Stem bark decoction is administered orally to treat infectious diseases such as sexually transmitted diseases (Magassouba et al., 2007). A. digitata is used for the treatment of fever, diarrhoea and haemoptysis
Precaution for Use	In hypertensive patient, the blood pressure should be monitored
Dosage and Dosage form	Decoction: 30 g of dried leaves is placed in 900 ml of water and is boiled until reduced to 600 ml. 1 teaspoon should be taken three times a day

3. Ageratum conyzoides

Botanical Name	Ageratum conyzoides
Common name	Australian Billy-goat weed, Goat weed, Mexican ageratum, Herbe de bouc (French).
Local name	Burkina Faso: Dioula – Chou kolan, Fulfuldé – Kikalapurél;kisalapuré Cote d'Ivoire: Baule – Kondre, Dan – Dussuo, Gagu – Maingue Gambia: Fula Pulaar – Chikara – Pre, Manding Mandinka – Hatayajambo Ghana: Akyem – Adwowakuro, Asante – Guakuro, Fante – Efumomoe Guinea Bissau: Crioulo – Balquiama, Fula – Laboel, Mandinka – Boro Guinea: Fula Pulaar – Kumba-Dongul

Liberia: Basa – Omalu-Ana, Mano – Dah Vo

Nigeria: Yuroba – Imi esu, Edo – Ebegho, Igbo – Ngwa

Senegal: Diola – Ekerkeda, Manding Bambara – Nun Gu, Wolof – Gobu

Sierra Leone: Kono – Yandigbene Yani, Krio – Wet-Ed-Lif, Susu Dyalonke-Khampu-Na.

Description	It is erect, branched, softly hispid, annual herb, may grow up to 1 m high; leaves opposite, arrangement decussate; ovate, setose-pubescent on nerves on lower surface, margin crenate, petiole slender, flower heads bluish-purple or whitish.
Habitat and Distribution	The plant grows widely in Northern Ghana and from Mali to Cameroon. It is commonly found in moist places or during rainy season in deserted villages and weedy areas including roadsides (Dokosi, 1998; GHP, 1992).
Plant part of interest	Fresh or dried leaf
Chemical constituents	Contains Volatile oil (eugenol); chromenes; triterpenoids including sterols; flavonoids and phenolic compounds (conyzorigun, 5-methoxynobiletin, quercetin, kaempferol glycosides); alkaloids; benzofurans and tannins (Okunade,

2002; GHP, 1992; Gill, 1978).

Ethnomedical Uses	In Africa, Asia and South America the plant is used for treating a wide variety of diseases including mental illness, headache, colic, skin ulcers, cuts and wounds, burns and dyspnoea. In Nigeria the decoction of the plant is taken internally to treat diarrhoea and intestinal pain. It is also incorporated into traditional soaps prepared from the ashes of plants such as cocoa (Theobroma cacao) and from palm kernel shafts (Elaeis guinensis). In Kenya it is used as an antiasthmatic, antispasmodic and haemostatic. In Brazilian medicine teas of conyzoides are taken as anti-inflammatory, analgesic, anti-diarrhoeic. In Vietnam it is used for gynaecologic complaints (Haensel et al, 1994; Durodola, 1977).
Precaution for use	Should be used with care in children and pregnant women.
Dosage and Dosage form	Decoction; Juice from bruised fresh leaves; Tincture; Capsules. Infusion: 20-30 g of dry leaves per litre of water; take 3-4 teacups day Decoction: 30-50 g per litre of water; take 3-4 teacups day Tincture: 1:5 30% fresh alcohol, take 2-5 ml twice daily Capsule: 1-2 g twice daily

4. Alchornea cordifolia

Botanical Name	Alchornea cordifolia
Common name	English: Christmas bush, French: Arbre de djeman, Alchornéa cordiforme
Local name	Burkina Faso: Dioula – kho sira;ko yira, Fulfuldé – Lahédi Cote d'Ivoire: Baoulé – Agni, Akyé – N'dzin, Malinké – Koyira Ghana: Akan – Ogyamma, Fante – Egyamma, Ga – Adangbe- Gboo Mali: Bambara – Kô gira, Malinké – Kogira, Peulh – Holâta, Bulora Nigeria: Hausa- Bambami, Igbo – Ububo, Yoruba – Ewe Ipa, Esinyin Senegal: Wolof- Lah, Diola- Purger yéné, Serer- Ardana, Yira

	Sierra Leone: Madingo – Yisai, Mende – Njekoi, Susu – Bolontha Togo: Ewé – Avovlo, Ouatchi – Avovlo
Description	It is a small tree or many stemmed, almost climbing shrub that can grow up to 5 – 8 m high; stem has blunt spines; leaves long-petiolate; broadly ovate, cordate at base, apex shortly acuminate. It has an entire or slightly dentate margin. Flowers are greenish-white in spikes or raceme; styles long and permanent on the fruit.
Habitat and Distribution	A. cordifolia is widely distributed throughout all countries of the West African region and across tropical Africa, in forests usually near water, moist or marshy places.
Plant part of interest	Leaf
Chemical constituents	Alkaloids (eg. alchornine and related alkaloids); tannins, flavonoids and proanthocyanidins are present (Bennet, 1950; Paris, 1958; Pruja, 1987; Ogundipe et al., 2001; Ayisi and Nyadedzor, 2003),
Ethnomedical Uses	It is commonly used in traditional medicine in Africa, together with other plants, and all the plants parts are used. The leaves are used in many African countries for the treatment of microbial, inflammatory, and stress

	related diseases. The roots are used against leprosy (Abbiw, 1990) and the leaf powder has wound and ulcer treatment properties (Kerharo and Bouquet, 1950). The plant is used to treat malaria in Mali and Cote d'Ivoire.
Precaution for use	Pregnancy, hypotension
Dosage and Dosage form	Decoction, tincture, infusion Decoction: 30-50 g of dried leaves per one liter of water; 3-4 teacups daily Infusion: 20-30 g of dried leaves per one liter of water; 3-4 teacups daily Tincture: 1:5, 45% ethanol; 5 ml three times daily

5. Allium sativum

Botanical Name	Allium sativum
Common name	Garlic (English); Ail commun (French)

Local name	Burkina Faso: Mooré – Gando;Layi, Dioula – Laii, Fulfuldé – Toumé Ghana: Twi – Gyene Kankan, Ga Adangbe – Aya, Hausa – Tafarmuwa
	Mali: Bambara – Tumé, Tamachek – Teskart
	Nigeria: Hausa – Tafárnúúwáá, Igbo – Oy Ayón, Ayún, Yoruba – Àlubósa, Ayúu
	Senegal: Wolof – Laji, Manding Bambara – Layi Togo: Ewe – Ayo, Nima – Ayo, Ouatchi – Ayo
Description	It is an erect, hardy and bulbous perennial herb up to 60 cm in height, with a central bulb covered in scales in the axil. The bulb consists of a number of cloves enclosed in a paper-like skin; leaves are long, flat and smooth. Leaf blade is cylindrical, hollow, linear, flat and solid with an acute apex.
Habitat and Distribution	Endemic to central Asia. Today, it is cultivated in many parts of the world, covering Europe, North Africa, Asia, and North America and the West African sub-region.
Plant part of interest	Bulb
Chemical constituents	Has volatile oil consisting mainly of sulfur-containing substances such as diallyl sulphide, alliin, allicine and

	alliinase (Gill, 1992), vitamins A, B, C, D and E, ajoenes (Chevallier, 1996), oleo-resins; amino acids; minerals (germanium, calcium, copper, iron, potassium, magnesium, selenium, zinc); saponin; cyanogenic glycosides; thioglycosides and flavonoids (GHP, 1992); amino acids; vitamins A, B, C and D (Newall et al)
Ethnomedical Uses	Garlic is cholesterol-lowering, antihypertensive, anti-coagulant, anti-diarrhoeal, anti-dysenteric. Also, used in treatment of fever, cough, flatulence, ulcer, hoarseness, bronchitis and other respiratory problems, skin diseases, burns, earache and tonsilitis, rheumatism, tuberculosis, typhoid, diabetes, arteriosclerosis, hyperlipidaemia as well as in the prevention of atherosclerotic (Elujoba and Olawode, 2004; Gill 1992; Adjanahoun et al., 1991),
Precaution for use	Garlic should be taken with food (Corzo-Martinez et al., 2007) because excessive doses, especially on an empty stomach, may cause stomach upsets, flatulence, heartburn, nausea and diarrhoea and changes in the intestinal flora.
Dosage and Dosage form	Intact bulb, decoction, tincture, tablets, capsules. Generally, the fresh bulb and the bulb oil can be given at 2-5 mg daily (or one fresh bulb or

clove 1-2 times daily) while the dose for the powder is at 400-1200 mg daily and tincture of 1:5 in 60% alcohol is given at 5 ml three times daily

6. Aloe schweinfurthii

Botanical Name	Aloe schweinfurthii
Common name	West African giant aloe, Elephant's palm fond
Local name	Ghana: Akan – Sereberebe, Brong – Nsesareso Abrobe
	Nigeria: Fula Fulfulde – Balli Nyibi, Yuroba – Eti eerin anago, Hausa – Hantsar Senegal: Bambara – Layi.
	Togo: Ewe – Adi adi
Description	It is a succulent and perennial herb. May have a short procumbent stem of about 20-40 cm long with small

bracts. It has a deflexed, greyish-green leaves with both surfaces spotted with whitish marks. The leaf is lanceolate, long with acute apex which may be about 60-80 cm long, 6-8 cm broad at the base. There is whitish teeth margin which is directed outwards the lower parts. The teeth, about 1 cm apart, turn red at maturity. stem 20-40 cm long. There is cylindrical racemes and sparsely branched inflorescence.

Habitat and Distribution

It is a perennial herb which is found in grassy places or moist savanna and its distribution covers Senegal, Nigeria, Central Africa, Zambia and Malawi. It is a suckering plant of rocky hillside in Ghana, Niger, Nigeria, Cameroons, Sudan and the Congo basin.

Plant part of interest

Whole leaf, yellow juice or the transparent colourless gel

Chemical constituents

The yellow exudate principally consists of phenolic compounds, which include the purgative anthracene derivatives e.g. aloin (Odeleye 2004).

Ethnomedical Uses

Used for treatment of conditions such as intestinal and urinogenital disorders. It is also applied on external body sores, wounds and burns. The sap is added to drinking water for poultry and is said to protect

	them against avian cholera. The edible flowers are sometimes used as a culinary in soups (Odeleye, 2004; Burkill, 1995; Hutchinson and Dalziel, 1958).
Precaution for use	Not to be taken on empty stomach
Dosage and Dosage form	Decoction: 30 g of dried leaves in 900 ml of water, boil until reduced to 600 ml, 1 teaspoon three times a day

7. Aloe vera

Botanical Name	Aloe vera
Common name	Curacao aloe, French; Aloés vulgaire
Local name	Burkina Faso: Kirma – Magno Gu Dondialé, Manding – Sinzé Toro,

Bambara – Sogobahu

Cote d'Ivoire: Manding – Sinzé Toro, Maninka – Bamalagba, Senufo Dyimini – Nimbéléké. Ghana: Akan – Sereberebe, Brong – Nsesareso Abrobe

Nigeria: Fula Fulfulde – Balli Nyibi Balli Nyiwa, Gwari – Omvi, Hausa – Zaabuwaa, Yoruba-eti eerin oyinbo

Senegal: Fula – Sogoba Hu, Bambara – Sogoba Bu, Maninka – Kadio Kandio.

Togo: Ewe – Adi Adi Gbe, Basari – Dissawede, Kabye – Sulefadium

Description
A. vera is a small rosette of fleshy succulent leaves growing from the center of the plant, with no distinct stem. It may grow to 30-40 cm in height. The thick, fleshy leaves are able to store large amounts of water during the rainy season and are therefore able to survive throughout the drought in the dry season. Influorescence is simple or branched and may either be terminal or lateral, with orange, red yellow or even white flowers.

Habitat and Distribution
It is a perennial herbaceous plant which is native to southern and eastern Africa, Arabian Peninsula, China, Gibraltar and Mediterranean countries. It is cultivated in Aruba,

	Bonaire, Maiti, India, South Africa, the United States of America and Venezuela and West Indies. It is also imported into some countries in Africa including West African sub-region where it is commonly grown in pots and flower beds.
Plant part of interest	Whole leaf, yellow juice or the transparent colourless gel
Chemical constituents	The plant contains phenolic compounds including anthraquinones and chromones; proteins, carbohydrate (Bruce, 1967; Lorenzett et al., 1964; Von Zyl and Viljoen, 2001).
Ethnomedical Uses	The plant is used in folkloric medicine to treat dermatitis, sun-burns, cystic ache, peptic ulcer, colds, tuberculosis, gonorrhoea, asthma, dysentery, headache, fungal infections and diabetes (Sample et al., 2001; WHO, 1991; Ali et al., 1990).
Precaution for use	Excessive or prolonged use of the plant material may cause nephritis, gastritis, vomiting and diarrhoea, stained with blood and mucus.
Dosage and Dosage form	Dried juice: 50-200mg orally for adults Decoction: two tablespoonfuls daily before meals.

8. Alstonia boonei

Botanical Name	Alstonia boonei
Common name	Pattern wood; stool wood, French; Emien
Local name	Burkina Faso: Fulfuldé – Moyatabél
	Cote d'Ivoire: Abe – Onguie Honguie, Baule – Emien Miei, Kulango – Senuro
	Ghana: Twi - Onyame Dua, Ga Adangbe – Sinu, Nzema – Nyamenlebaka
	Guinea: Fula Pulaar – Leguere, Kissi – Tiendo, Loma – Zolo
	Guinea-Bissau: Fula Pulaar – Bantera-Foro, Manding Mandinka– Bantam-Foro (D'o)
	Liberia: Dan – Yung, Kru Guere

	(Krahn) – GonaTu
	Nigeria: Edo – Ukhu, Engenni – Uguwa, Igbo – Egbu, Yoruba-ahun Senegal: Banyun – Ti Keung, Diola – Bain, Fula Pulaar – Ataforo. Sierra Leone: Mende – Kalo Wulo
	Togo: Ewe – Nyami dua, Ouatchi – tonton, Mina - siaketekre
Description	It is a deciduous tree and can grow up to 35 m high. It has buttresses deep-fluted high and narrow. Leaves are in whorls at nodes; oblanceolate, apex rounded to acuminate with prominent lateral veins almost at right angles to midrib. Flowers are white, fruits are paired and has slender follicles up to 16 cm long.
Habitat and Distribution	The plant is found in the forest zones of Ghana and throughout tropical Africa
Plant part of interest	Stem bark.
Chemical constituents	Alkaloids (echitamine, echitamidine, alstonine, alstonidine); triterpenoids (lupeol, ursolic acid, βamyrin); tannins; iridoids (boonein, loganin); minerals (calcium, phosphorus, iron, sodium, potassium, and magnesium); ascorbic acid (Ojewole, 1984; Iwu,

1993).

Ethnomedical Uses	Used in West and Central Africa for the treatment of malaria, fever, intestinal helminthes, rheumatism and hypertension. Stem bark is used in treatment of malaria, asthma and impotence. In Ghana, is given for toothache and to women after delivery to aid in expelling the placenta Infusion of the bark is used as antivenom for snake bites. it is also used in treating painful micturation and rheumatic conditions (Abel and Busia, 2005; Betti, 2004; Sofowora, 1993; Asuzu and Anaga, 1991)
Precaution for use	Crude drugs containing alkaloids must be taken with care.
Dosage and Dosage form	Decoction: 30-50 g per litre of water; drink 3-4 cups a day. Tincture: 1:5 in 45% alcohol; take 5 ml three times daily

9. Argemone Mexicana

Botanical Name	Argemone Mexicana
Common name	Mexican poppy, Prickly poppy, Mexican prickly, Yellow poppy, Yellow thistle, Mexican thistle (English). Pivot épineux, Pavot du Mexique, tache de l'œil, Chardon du pays (French
Local name	Ghana: Akan- Akusiribie, Twi- Kokosakyi aduro
	Mali: Bambara- Bozobo, Dogon- Aignètawa, Sonkeriai, Senoufo- Naka - taba Senegal: Wolof- Garabu-mag, Diola- Fambora, Serer- Dahatu Fa N'Gol
	Togo: Adja- Houétchègnon

Description	The plant is an annual herb with a woody base. It is erect, reaching 1 m in height and has branches. Leaves are alternate and sessile, with lobed and serrated edge, teeth are tipped with prickly spikes, ribs are alternate, thorns on the lower limb. The flowers are terminal and can reach 2.5 to 5 cm in diameter with green sepals and bright yellow petals. Fruits are ovoid capsules, rectangular with numerous spines erect or spreading; latex is yellow while the seed is dark brown, round and clear.
Habitat and Distribution	As the name implies, the plant is native to Mexico but is today, found in many tropical countries of both northern and southern hemispheres. The plant is widespread throughout Africa and occurs irregularly in the SudanoSahelian zone of West Africa
Plant part of interest	Aerial parts without seeds, leaf
Chemical constituents	Some of its chemical components inchude coumarins, mucilage, sterols, tannins, benzoquinones, triterpenes and alkaloids, fat, organic acids (tartaric acid, succinic acid, citric acid and malic acid), combined and free amino acids, monosaccharides (glucose and fructose) and minerals, and vitamin C; flavonoids (Singh et al. 2011; Rahman and Ilyas, 1961).

Ethnomedical Uses	Leaves are used in treatment of enteralgia, gonorrhoea, constipation, muscle pain, jaundice and liver malfunction, uncomplicated malaria, cough, toothache, eye pain, urethral discharge, hepatobiliary disorders, bilious, fevers, eczema, and haematuria. The juice is used as a sedative and antiemetic. It is also applied in the treatment of ear infections and eye diseases. Infused seeds and the aerial part as well are used as diuretic, purgative and diaphoretic. The oil is used in constipation, insomnia, skin infections and sores
Precaution for use	Do not use beyond one week
Dosage and Dosage form	Decoction Leaf powder: 30 g in 500 ml of water for 30 min. Taken twice a day

10. Azadirachta indica

Botanical Name	Azadirachta indica
Common name	Neem, Indian lilac; Margosa tree; Nim, French: Margousier;Nîm
Local name	Burkina Faso: Mooré – Niim, Dioula – Nîmyiri, Fula Fulfuldé – Tirotiya;Goodji
	Cote d'Ivoire: Akye – Djé Ndédzakoè , Ando' – Tchitchèndé Gambia: Manding Mandinka – Yirinding Kunango
	Ghana: Twi – Dua Gyane, Ewe – Liliti, Hausa – Dongo Yaro Mali: Bambara –
	Mali yirini, Senoufo – Gnimitigue, Dyula – Goo-gay
	Niger: Hausa - Dogon Yaro, Songhai – Méli, Djerma - Milleize. Nigeria:

	Hausa – Dogonyaro, Kanuri – Gányá Nîm, Yoruba – Dongoyaro
	Senegal: Manding Mandinka – Tubabo toboro, Soce-tubabo, Wolof – Dim dim i buki
	Togo: Ewe – Sabuleti, Mina – Kiniti, Adja – Sablagbe
Description	It is a tree that may grow straight over 20 m high, and has a striped and fissured bark. Has alternate and paripinnate leaves with about 5-8 pairs of leaflets at the base. Inflorescence in axillary panicles white flowers which are numerous and are borne on pedicels of about 1.5 mm long with sepals ovate-sub orbicular. Oblanceolated petals are white of 5 to 6 mm long. Anthers are found within lobe apex. Fruits are ellipsoid and ovoid shape, one-seeded, and become yellow when ripe. The plant may survive up to about 200 years.
Habitat and Distribution	It is a tropical tree which originated from India and Burma. It grows in Southeast Asia and West Africa and it prevail in northern and southern parts of Nigeria so also in the coastal and Northern Savanna areas of Ghana. Now cultivated in the Caribbean and parts of Central America. The plant can grow even without watering especially in arid and semi-arid regions and in poor sandy

	or stony soil.
Plant part of interest	Leaf
Chemical constituents	Consists of alkaloids, stigmasterol, tannins, flavonoids/polyphenols, saponins and sugar, Vitamin C. Triterpenes/meliaceous/limonoid compounds, azadirachtin, nimbolide, gedunin, salanin, other meliacins; diterpenes; carotenoids, reducing sugars and fixed oil present
Ethnomedical Uses	Indica is used for the treatment of nausea, vomiting, fever, malaria, cough, jaundice, gonorrhoea, eczema intestinal worm infestation, skin disorders, boils, ulcers, and leprosy in indigenous system of medicine
Precaution for use	Caution should be taken in the administration of the aqueous extract in liver and renal disease. Neem extracts should not be taken for prolonged periods at high doses
Dosage and Dosage form	Decoction: 30 g dried leaves in 900 ml water; simmer until reduced to 600 ml; 1 teacup three times daily; tincture- 1:5 in 45% alcohol, 5 ml three times daily Liquid extract 1:2 in 45% alcohol, 2.5 ml three times daily

11. Balanites aegyptiaca

Botanical Name	Balanites aegyptiaca
Common name	Soap berry tree, Thorn tree (English); Desert date, Dattier du désert (French)
Local name	Burkina Faso: Mooré – kyéguelga, Dioula – Zèkènè, Fulfulde – Tannê;yoléteki Ghana: Dagaare – Gongo Mali: Bambara – Zèkènè; Dogon – Mono, Noms – Tale Senegal: Wolof – Sump; Serer – Model, lol; Arabe – Hadjlidj Togo: Gourmantche – Konkonlangpag; Moba – Okopakbo
Description	The tree has thorns over it surface and is deciduous which may grow up to 8 metres high, with complex branching pattern. It well defined trunk may be straight or slightly twisted with a greyish-brown bark that is fissured longitudinally. Inflorescence is indeterminate, comprises of 5 to 12 flowers arranged on a pubescent stem,

	of variable length. It has a fleshy drupe fruits of 1 to 2.5 cm long, which is normally oval oblong, with silky-pubescent surface and greenish-white with a single seed inside.
Habitat and Distribution	The desert date palm grows well in sandy soil and on all types of geographical landscapes. It is found mainly in tropical Africa, especially in central and Western Sahara, and the Far East. It originated from the Mediterranean via Egypt.
Plant part of interest	Fruit and stem bark
Chemical constituents	Protein, carbohydrates (Nour et al., 1986); saponins (balanitin-3, 6-methyldiosgenin, balanitoside; (Kamel 1998; Hosny et al., 1992), pregnane glycosides
Ethnomedical Uses	The leaves and fruits of desert date palm as well as edible oil extracted from its kernels are consumed as food during the dry season. The leaves when dried and processed into powder are use in preparing sauce (Cook et al., 1998; Lockett et al., 2000). The fruit extract is added to porridge and eaten by nursing mothers to stimulate lactation of milk, while the nuts are eaten to treat pain and discomfort associated with intestine. The seeds are used to treat cancers and hydrocoele (Abubakar et al., 2007).

	The stem and root barks are powdered and mixed with other species, and then boiled with water for use against oral candidiasis. . The root bark is crushed, added to water, soaked and drunk for its purgative effect. Similarly, the stem bark is soaked in warm water, and then the extract is taken for asthma, dry cough and chest infections. Leaves is taken as tea to treat uterine fibroids (Tabuti et al., 2003), and may be processed as paste and applied to bleeding gums or inserted into the cavity of painful tooth three times per day until recovery. The leaves of the plant and young branches are macerated and applied fresh as poultice on wounds and can also used as a bath to treat measles.
Precaution for use	The blood glucose level of the patient should be controlled.
Dosage and Dosage form	Decoction: 30-50 g per litre of water; take 3-5 teacupful daily Tincture: 1:5 in 50% alcohol; 5 ml three times a day.

12. Bridelia ferruginea

Botanical Name	Bridelia ferruginea
Common name	Bridelia
Local name	Benin: Baatonun- Bemebenku, Gbe Fo – Honsukokué , Yoruba – Nago Hira
	Burkina Faso: Mooré – Ambriaka, Dioula– sagoui;sagwann baboni, Fulfuldé–kojuteki;daafi
	Cote d'Ivoire: Manding Maninka– Saba / Sagba, Senufo– Dyimini – Nakurugo
	Ghana: Tw – Opam fufuo, Ga Adamgbe – Flatsho, Hausa– Kisni Guinea: Fula Pulaar – Dafi, Manding Maninka– Baboni, Maninka– Sagba
	Mali: Bambara – Saguan, Noms – Daafi, Senoufo – Gnirin-o-tigue Nigeria: Yoruba – Ira odan, Eepo ira;

	Ibo – Oha, Hausa – Kisni
	Sierra Leone: Susu – Tholinyi, Kissi – Sindio, Hono – Bembeh Togo: Ewe – Akamati, Bassar – N'tchintchi, Lamba – Kolu
Description	It is a small, scaly tree or shrub that grows to about 4-15 m tall and to 1.5 m in diameter. Branching is low, often bears spines and may be slash crimson coloured. The leaves may be small to medium-sized, simple, petiolate with stipules, oval-lanceolate, alternate or sometimes sub-alternately, spiral, with lamina broadly elliptic, and margin is entire. (GHP, 1992). Also the leaf is pinnately veined, which form a dense and prominent network of veins, and sometimes hair may obscure the undersurface of the leaf. Inflorescence is made up of many flowers which are axillary and very dense.
Habitat and Distribution	The plant prevails in the Guinea savannah and coastal plains of Africa, especially Burkina Faso, Ghana, Nigeria and Togo as well as Asia and Australia
Plant part of interest	Leaf and stem-bark
Chemical constituents	The plant is rich in Flavonoids (bridelilactone and bridelilactoside, apigenin and kaempferol, gallocatechin. triterpenes, steroids,

	tannins, saponins; triterpenoids, lignans; phenols and tannins (Cimanga et al., 2001, Rashid et al., 2000; Irobi et al., 1994; GHP, 1992; de-Bruyne et al., 1998; Oliver-Bever, 1960).
Ethnomedical Uses	It is used to treat bacterial infections, malaria fever in children, mycotic stomatitis, dysentery, diabetes, arthritis, bruises, boils, dislocation, burns, dysentery, diabetes. It is also used as antidote for snake bites, treatment of gonorrhoea, helminthiasis, trypanosomes, inflammations sexually transmitted diseases (Okpekon et al., 2004; Irobi et al., 1994; Narayan, 1994; Iwu, 1993; Hentchoya, 1991; OliverBever,1960; Dalziel, 1937).
Precaution for use	Care should be taken in the administration of the aqueous extract in patients with liver and renal related problems.
Dosage and Dosage form	Infusion: 20 g of dried leaf per litre of water; brew for 15 minutes and take 3-4 cups a day; Decoction: boil 30 g of dried leaf in one litre of water for 15 minutes; drink 3-5 cups a day; Tincture: 1:5 in 30% alcohol; 5 ml three times daily

13. Carica papaya

 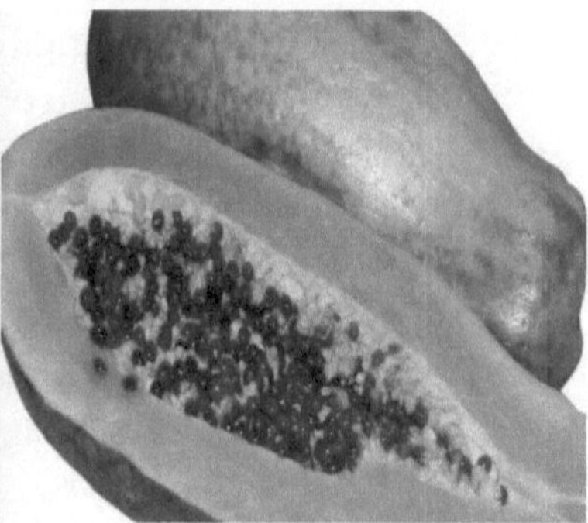

Botanical Name	Carica papaya
Common name	Pawpaw; melon tree, mummy apple, Papaya (English), Papayer (French)
Local name	Burkina Faso: Bissa – Nassara-krou, Mossi – P apaï, Moore– Budebalod;bogfiré,Fulfuldé- Mãndjé
	Cote d'Ivoire: Abbey – Oloko, Akye - M'bomou, baoule – Oflè Gambia: Mandinka – Papiya, Fulla – Budi baga, Wollof – Papakayo Ghana: Akan – Brofre, Ga-Dangbe – Akpakpa, Ewe – Adiba
	Mali: Bambara – Mandje, Dogons – Ane sara kambe, Senoufo – Manli
	Nigeria: Hausa – Gwanda, gwadda, Yoruba – Igi-Ibepè; Ibo – ogede ojo.
	Togo: Ewe – Adibati, Mina – Adubati, Akasselem – Brofude

	Senegal: Wolof – Papayo, Peuhl – papaya, papayo, Diola – bum papa Sierra leone: Mandigo – Sida, Mende – Fakali, Hono – Sela
Description	It is a straight, unbranched, soft-wooded tree of up to 5-6 m high with numerous leaf scars on a surface of a hollow stem. It has large palmate leaves may reach a metre in diameter and are organised at the top of the stem. The leaf petiole is long and hollow. Inflorescences are axillary cymes and the flowers are white or greenish, dioecious, unisexual in nature. Also, the flowers are occasionally hermaphrodite. In the unisexual nature, the male flowers are gamopetalous and tassel while the female flowers are large, polypetalous and sub-sessile. The fruits are oblong or oblong oval which may grow up to 30 cm long and 7-11 cm wide with fleshy mesocarp, yellow or gold when ripe and green when unripe
Habitat and Distribution	The plant is native to tropical America and is cultivated in homes and gardens in many other tropical regions of the world. It is less commonly grown in the Sahel.
Plant part of interest	Leaf, fruit or root
Chemical	Phenyl-propanoids, alkaloids, cyanogenic glucoside (Nahrstedt,

constituents	1987), alkaloids, carpaine, nicotine, xylitol and saponins, carotenoids, lycopene, annins; αlinolenic acid, benzenoid, benzaldehyde, benzyl glucosinolate, methyl salicylate, sulfur compounds, isothiocyanate benzyl, protein, papain, chimopapaine A, ω-protease, vitamins A, C and E2, minerals: potassium, mainly calcium, iron, phosphorus, sterols and fatty acids (Tang, 1971; Moneret et al., 1985; Kermanshai et al., 2001; Hashem et al., 1980; Duke and Atchley, 1986; Kerharo and Adam, 1974).
Ethnomedical Uses	The fresh or dried leaves are used to treat febrile illness. The leaf decoction is used to treat cancer, malaria, urogenital pain and gonorrhoea. Asthma is treated using fumes from the leaves. Paste made from the root is dissolved in warm water and used as an enema to treat abdominal pain. It is also mixed with palm oil and used as a poultice to treat whitlow. Dental caries is treated using the root macerated in cold water. The macerated roots and leaves are also used orally against diuretics, urethritis (painful urination), typhoid, fever, and as a laxative. The roots may also be macerated in palm wine or decocted and drunk to treat dysentery and gonorrhoea. The decoction of the unripe fruit is also used in treatment for jaundice, sickle cell anaemia and hepatitis (African

	Pharmacopoeia, 1985; Ake Asse, 2001)
Precaution for use	Papain is thought to have the ability to dissolve the protein responsible for implantation of the fertilized egg in the lining of the uterus and therefore, may cause abortion in early pregnancy.
Dosage and Dosage form	Latex Decoction: 30 g of dried leaves in 900 ml of water and is boiled until reduced to 600 ml. Then, 1 teaspoonful should be taken three times a day.
	Infusion: 30 g of dried leaves is dissolved in 600 ml of water. And 1 teaspoonful is taken three times a day.
	1:5 tincture in alcohol 50% 5 ml times a day.
	Latex: 10-20 g mixed with honey and warm water after every meal. The fresh latex of green fruit, with a dose of 4 to 8 g (1 to 2 tablespoons for children) and 8 to 16 g (2 to 4 tablespoons for adults), diluted in a little water, or mixed with 3 or 4 tablespoons of honey.

14. Cinchona pubescens

Botanical Name	Cinchona pubescens
Common name	Quinine (English), Quinquina/quinine rouge (French)
Local name	Nigeria: Yoruba – Kinin
Description	It may be larger shrubs or small tree that can reach the size of 15-20 m high. It has leaves which are opposite, rounded to lanceolate that are 10 – 40 cm long. The tree produces white, pink, or yellow flowers in terminal panicles. Fruits are small capsule containing numerous seeds.
Habitat and Distribution	The plant originated from South America, and was introduced and cultivated in the humid tropics of Africa and Madagascar (African Pharmacopoeia, 1985).
Plant part of interest	Dried stem bark

Chemical constituents	Quinine, quininidine, cinchonine and cinchonidine (African Pharmacopoeia, 1985). Also rich in cuscamidine, caffeic acid, cinchophyllamine, cinchotannic acid, xaricine, conquinamine, aricine, cuscamine, cusconidine, javanine, paricine, proanthocyanidins, quinacimine, quinamine, quinic acid, quinicine, quinovic acid, quinovine and sucirubine
Ethnomedical Uses	Quinine, obtained from the bark, was first proposed for sale in England in 1658 and was made official in the British Pharmacopoeia in 1677. The cinchona bark was included in many formulations in Europe, such as "Countess's powder", "Jesuit's powder". Besides malaria, the bark was also used to treat fever, indigestion, diseases of the mouth and throat, and cancer.
Precaution for use	Alkaloid containing drugs must be administered with caution
Dosage and Dosage form	The right doses of plant material depend on several factors such as the user's age, health, and several other conditions

15. Cryptolepis sanguinolenta

Figure 2. *Cryptolepis sanguinolenta* plants in flower 105 DAP (arrow pointing to an unopened flower).

Botanical Name	Cryptolepis sanguinolenta
Common name	Ghana quinine; yellow – dye root, French;Quinine du Ghana
Local name	Cote d'Ivoire: Anyi – Alui Okle Ghana: Twi – Nibima, Ewe – Kadze, Hausa – Gangaman Guinea Bissau: Banyan – Konit, Diola – Fu Lemok, Vulgar Balanta – Butnacimbore
	Guinea: Fula Pulaar – Delboi, Manding Bambara – Uiduloia, Maninka – Nombon
	Nigeria: Hausa – Gangamaa, Igbo (Ogwashi) – Kpolokoto
	Senegal: Balanta–Butnasimbor, Diola Flup– Ahayte Buka Ka, Bambara – Vidukokoy
	Sierra Leone: Koranko – Firabantikpa, Mende – Kpokoyangole
	Togo: Ewe – Kedze, Ouatchi –

Anotsidzen, Mina – Kadzen.

Description	It a shrub that has a thin stem that twinned. Its leaves are elliptic, oblong-elliptic, with acute apex and symmetrical base, petiolate, which is up to 7 cm long and 3 cm wide. Inflorescence cyme, which is lateral on branch shoots with few flowers. The corolla tube is up to 5 mm long and yellow in colour. The fruits have pair of follicles with seeds having long silky hairs. The plant when dried is having sweet-scent and the root has a bitter taste.
Habitat and Distribution	The plant is indigenous to Africa and can be found in places such as Central, Eastern, and Western Africa (Tona et al., 1998). It commonly grows in scattered open spaces, mostly among forest clearings (GHP, 1992)
Plant part of interest	Root
Chemical constituents	The plant contains cryptolepine, quindoline, a phenolic derivative of cryptolepine and two other uncharacterised alkaloids (Addy, 2003; Bierer et al., 1998; Dwuma-Badu et al., 1978; Gellert et al., 1951).
Ethnomedical Uses	Aqueous extract from cryptolepis is used by traditional healers in Guinea-Bissau to cure jaundice and hepatitis

<table>
<tr><td></td><td>(Oliver-Bever, 1986). Infusions of the roots are used in the treatment of stomach and intestinal disorders in Zaire and the Casamance district of Senegal (Silva et al., 1996; Kerharo and Adam, 1974). In Ghana, powder of the dried root is boiled in water, are used in treating various forms of fever, malaria, urinary respiratory tract infections, rheumatism and venereal diseases. Congolese traditional medicine practitioners use the aqueous decoction of the root bark in the treatment of amoebiasis (Boye, 1989).</td></tr>
<tr><td>Precaution for use</td><td>Avoid driving or operating machinery instantly after taking the plant extract. Aqueous extract should not be administered to a pregnant woman.</td></tr>
<tr><td>Dosage and Dosage form</td><td>Infusion: 2.5g teabag of root bark soaked in 150 ml (1 cup) of boiling water; steep for 5-10 minutes (Boye, 2002).

Decoction: 40 g per litre of water, 3-5 teacupfuls daily.

Tincture: 1:5 in 45% alcohol, 5 ml three times daily</td></tr>
</table>

16. Cymbopogon citratus

Botanical Name	Cymbopogon citratus
Common name	English: Fever herb; Citronnelles, Lemon grass. French: Citronelle, verveine des indes
Local name	Burkina Faso: Dioula – Bin boulou;citroneli, Fulfuldé – Wuluundé Gambia: Manding Mandinka – Kanyang Yallo Ghana: Fante – Ti-Ahaban, Ga-Adangbe – Ti-Ba, Ewe – Tighe. Guinea: Konyagi – I-Dɛl Tɛgag Guinea-Bissau: Crioulo – Belgata, Mali: Bambara– Bin boulou, Senoufo–Cafi- gna Nigeria: Ibibio – Myoyaka Makara, Igbo (Owerri) – Achara Ehi, Yoruba – Kooko Oba. Sierra Leone: Bulom(Kim) – Pei-Poto, Kono – Pu-

	Lumbi, Mendu – Pu-Lumbe.
	Senegal: Bambara – cè kala
	Togo: Ewe– Tsigbe, Ouatchi– Gbehoin, Mina – Fifaglass
Description	The plant is an aromatic perennial herb that may grow to 2 m high or more. It rarely make flowering, but robust with odoriferous, aromatic light green leaves that are borne on adventitious roots. There is lower glumes of sessile spikelet which are narrowly lanceolate, almost flat to deeply concave, with the bottom of the depression rounded and wingless at the apex. Leaf-blades which narrow at the base are linear to filiform in shape. The leaves are 70 cm long and 5 – 15 mm broad taped at the ends and are fragrant. Margins are scabrous with prominent midrib underneath; inflorescence is in panicles (Burkill, 1985).
Habitat and Distribution	The herb is native to tropical Asia and cultivated in homes as medicinal aromatic herb. Sometimes, it is grown as an ornamental plant in compounds, along roadsides and also embankments and on hillsides to check erosion
Plant part of interest	Fresh or dried leaf
Chemical	Contains volatile oil constituents (e.g.

constituents	cymbopogone, cymbopogonol, citral, geraniol, citronellal), alkaloids, saponins, flavonoids, tannins and simple sugars (Onabanjo et al., 1993
Ethnomedical Uses	The plant is used diuretic, antimalarial, stomachic tonic, antiseptic; anxiolytic, hypnotic; anticonvulsant, hypotensive, anticatarrhal and antiheumatic in African Traditional Medicine (African Pharmacopoiea, 1985, Oliver, 1959). It is used treatment for cough, sprains, ringworm, athlete's foot; malaria, fever, jaundice, throat and chest infections. It can equally be used for moderate-to-severe pain, hypertension, diabetes mellitus, obesity, nervous and gastrointestinal disturbances (Adeneye and Agbaje, 2007; Blanco et al., 2007; Tchoumbougnang et al., 2005; Onabanjo et al., 1993; Gill, 1992; Carlini et al., 1986).
Precaution for use	The volatile oil sourced from the plant qhich is obtained by steam distillation of the fresh leaves is used as flavouring agent or as antimicrobial drug preparation, and it must be regulated to prevent possible toxicity.
Dosage and Dosage form	Decoction: 30 g dried herb in 900 ml water, simmer until it reduced to 600 ml. Then, 1 teacup should be taken three times daily.

Infusion: 30 g dried herb is put in 600 ml of water. Then, 1 teacup should be taken three times daily.

Tincture: 1:5 in 45% alcohol, 5 ml three times daily.

17. Euphorbia hirta

Botanical Name	Euphorbia hirta
Common name	Australian asthma herb, Queensland asthma weed, pills bearing spurge, cat's hair, milkweed, Hairy spurge (English), Euphorbe hérissée;petit euphorbe (French)
Local name	Burkina Faso: Moore – Wal-biisum, Fulafulde – Intan boũgâdjé; èn èngil, Dioula – Ntugansin
	Cote d'Ivoire: Baule – Adododo, Gagu – Tao Moa, Kru Bete – Blableg-Ware Ghana: Akan – Kakaweadwe,

Ewe – Notsigbe, Nzema – Aakuba

Guinea-Bissau: Fula Pulaar – Taquelpolhe Liberia: Mano – To A Gbondo Mali: Dogon – Peleguere Djimi, Bambara – Dabadaba Bileni Nigeria: Yoruba–Emile, irawo'le,Fula Fulfulde– Endamyel, Hausa– Noonon Kurciyaa

Senegal: Badyara – Makoreselu, Diola Flup – Ku Tim, Fula Pulaar – En Engil Sierra Leone: Limba – Fuŋkele, Loko – Bumbuŋgo, Mende-Bɛlɛji

Togo: Ewe – Anonsikan, Akasselem – Melandjebe, Ouatchi – Nostika

Description The plant is herbaceous, erect or prostrate, slender that often grows close to the ground. It is 20 – 40 cm high and pubescent. It has annual stems, some of which are perennial. The stem is covered with yellowish bristly hairs, especially in the younger parts. There are reddish-purple patches on the older partsof the plant body. Leaves are all opposite, usually obviously unequal at the base. The leaves are obliquely ovate to lanceolate and rounded on one side. And oblong-obovate 2 to 5 cm long, 2 cm wide. Inflorescence is in axillary tufts and terminal glomerulus and contains small yellowish male or bisexual flower. Fruits are small,

	yellowish, hairy and have three-celled capsules about of about 1 mm in diameter.
Habitat and Distribution	It is among the common weed that occurs near drains, roadsides and waste places in towns and villages. It is indigenous to India and most tropical countries of the world
Plant part of interest	Fresh or dried leaf or aerial tops
Chemical constituents	Diterpenes, triterpenes, flavonoids (quercitrin, quercitol, myriscitrin); hydrolysable tannins (euphorbins A-E); aromatic acids (shikimic and related acids); alkaloids, coumarins, anthocyanins and saponins (GHP, 1992).
Ethnomedical Uses	It is the most effective that is used in the treatment scorpion sting, fever, cough, bronchial and paroxysmal asthma, amoebic dysentery, hay fever and worm infestations (NHP, 2008). In China, the plant is used to treat dysentery, athlete's foot and other skin conditions.
Precaution for use	Care should be taken in the administration of the aqueous extract in patients with compromised liver function and the unconfirmed carcinogenic effect due to the content of phorbol esters.
Dosage and	Decoction; infusion; juice from fresh

Dosage form	leaves; liquid extract; tincture. Infusion: 20-30 g of dried plant per litre of water; drink 3-4 cups daily. Decoction: 30-50 g of dried leaves; drink 3-4 cups daily. Liquid extract (BPC 1949): 1:1 in 45% alcohol; 0.12-0.3ml three times a day. Tincture (BPC 1923): 1:5 in 60% alcohol, take 0.6-2ml three times a day.

18. Hallea stipulosa

Botanical Name	Hallea stipulosa
Common name	African linden, Abura (English); Tilleul d'Afrique, Bahia (French)
Local name	Ghana: Akan – Subaha Akoa, Nzema – Baya
	Guinea Conakry: Pular – Maninka Kouranko, Pöpö – Soussou Föfè, Kissi – Pawe Liberia: Kru – Boh

	Senegal: Diola – Bubagala
Description	H. stipulosa is a tree of up to 15 – 20 m tall and with cylindrical shaft without buttresses. It may grow the thickness of up to 1 m in diameter forms a very thick and scaly bark. It has a dense crown with several tufts and has broad, simple, opposite, slightly leathery, elliptical leaves measuring around 10 to 50 cm long. Inflorescence composed of several small globular flowers which are tight white calyx. And the fruit when formed is small spherical capsules. The plant has tap root system.
Habitat and Distribution	These are the kinds that grow in an area that is periodically flooded, savannas or near temporary ponds. They also occur in tropical Africa (Guinea, Senegal, Mauritania, Cameroon, Chad, Sudan).
Plant part of interest	Stem bark and leaf
Chemical constituents	The plant contains triterpenes as well as α-amyrin, quinovic acid--3-O-β-Dquinovopyranoside-27-O-β-D-glucopyranosyl. It is also rich in ursolic acid, quinovic acid, quinovin C glycoside, acid-3-O-acetyl-β ursolic. There are quinovic-acid-3-O-β-Dglucopyranoside, zygophyloside B, oleanolic acid, zygophyloside D and daucosterol (Fatima et al. 2002;

	Tapondju et al., 2002
Ethnomedical Uses	The bark is used for the treatment of gonorrhoea in Cote d'Ivoire. (Bouquet and Debray, 1974). In Guinea the decoction of the stem bark is used as a diuretic and antiseptic. The infusion is used to treat infertility especially in females. The leaves are used as topical antiseptic for wounds (Magassouba et al., 2007). In Ghana, the decoction of the dried stem bark, administered orally is very effective against Guinea worm (Comley, 1990). The decoction is used to treat malaria in adults (Kohler et al., 2002), while the bark is used for the treatment of genital, urinary and worm infestations (Adjahonoun et al., 1974; Wome, 1985).
Precaution for use	The recommended doses should be strictly adhered to.
Dosage and Dosage form	Decoction: 30 g of dried plant material be put in 900 ml water and boil until it reduced to 600 ml. Then, two tablespoonfuls should be taken three times daily

19. Harrisonia abyssinica

Botanical Name	Harrisonia abyssinica
Common name	Baingou (French)
Local name	Ghana: Asante – Fintinko,
	Guinea Conakry: Kpèlè – Zhinwuon Nyegolo
	Cote d'Ivoire: Anyi – Baingu Nigeria: Hausa – Arujere
	Sierra Leone: Kissi – Mama Kundu
	Togo: Ewe – Xedja, Mina – Hedjan, Adja – Xedjatsi
Description	Ghana: Asante – Fintinko,
	Guinea Conakry: Kpèlè – Zhinwuon Nyegolo
	Cote d'Ivoire: Anyi – Baingu
	Nigeria: Hausa – Arujere

	Sierra Leone: Kissi – Mama Kundu
	Togo: Ewe – Xedja, Mina – Hedjan, Adja – Xedjatsi
Habitat and Distribution	Dry evergreen forest patches or xerophytic (in Savannah). It is often found in coastal regions
Plant part of interest	Leaf or stem bark
Chemical constituents	It contains steroids: sitosterol, stigmasterol and campesterol. And also poriferasterol, stigmastenone, stigmastatrienone and sitostenone. Friedelanone: methylcholestenone; cycloabyssinone (Balde et al., 2000). There are also limonoids, obacunone, harrisonine, acetoxyharrisonine, diacetoxyharrisonine, pedonine, atalantolide and dehydroriciopsine (Okorie, 1982; Rajab et al., 1997, 1999; Chabbra et al., 1984).
Ethnomedical Uses	The powdered of the root bark and root decoction is used cure venereal diseases, malaria, diarrhoea, intestinal worms, urinary diseases, gonorrhea, stomach and tooth ache. Grinded dried Leaves with seeds of Aframomum melegueta, kaolin and salt is effective against vaginal discharge. The roots of the plant are chewed with palm kernel as an aphrodisiac (Balde, 1990), while the root decoction is used against gonorrhoea, tuberculosis and

	schistosomiasis. The decoction of young roots is effective against dizziness, insomnia, nausea, vomiting, orchitis and tuberculosis. The decoction may also cause abortion (Kirira et al., 2006; Hassanali et al., 1987).
Precaution for use	Do not exceed the stated doses
Dosage and Dosage form	Decoction: 30 g of dried plant material in 900 ml water; boil until reduced to 600 ml; two tablespoonfuls three times daily

20. Hibiscus sabdariffa

Botanical Name	Hibiscus sabdariffa
Common name	Red Sorrel, Karkade, Roselle, Hibiscus, Sudan tea, Zobo (English), l'Oiselle de Guinée, thé rose d'Abyssinie, oseille rouge (French)

Local name	Burkina Faso: Bobo – Yoro, Fulfuldé – Follere; pôllê, Dioula – Dah wiléni, Mooré – bito ou wegderé
	Gambia: Fula Pulaar – Foleray, Manding Mandinka – Dawaso, Wolof – Bissab Ghana: Dagbani – Dibemre, Hausa –Yakuwa, Konkomba – Tingyanbam
	Guinea: Basari – Yamen, Fula Pulaar – Folere Ba Di, Konyagi – Yavetyan
	Guinea-Bissau: Balanta – Mbatu, Crioulo – Baguiche, Manding Mandinka - Cutcha Mali: Dogon – Handjibane, Bambara – Dah Bileni, Senoufo – Tangnire
	Niger: Dende – Jisima, Songhai – Jisima
	Nigeria: Fula Fulfulde – Dorongu, Hausa – Abin Kan, Yoruba – Amukan, isapa
	Senegal: Vulgar – Bassap, Tukulor – Folerebadi, Bambara – Da Kumu
	Sierra Leone: Bulom – Satoɛ, Koranko – Dagbami, Krio – Sakpa Togo: Ewe – Anyegba, Mina – Gnatu, Kabye – Gnotu
Description	This is an annual plant found in the tropical regions of the world. It is 150–210 cm tall and make a broad clump of branches from its base. It

	has a lobed, reddish leaves and stems. It has a fleshy calyx that is red in colour and has acidic taste which is normally harvested before it develops into a woody matter. The calyx is the part that is left over after the bloom. Its leaves are 3-lobed, ovate in shape, undivided and is normally broad and crenate-serrate or dendate The stems are within the range of 7.2-9.6 cm long.. Flowers are developed as axillary, solitary and nearly sessile. On the flower, the corolla is yellow and is twice as long as its thickness. Fruits formed are ovoid, pubescent and is within the range of 1.2-1.8 cm long (GHP, 2007).
Habitat and Distribution	Hibiscus sabdariffa originates from Southeast Asia, some African countries that include Sudan and Egypt. It also grows well in the savanna areas of Nigeria from which the beverage called "zobo" is made and taken as a drink.
Plant part of interest	Calyx and calyculus
Chemical constituents	The plant contains tannin, anthocyanin (delphinidin and cyanidin), iron, calcium, zinc; aluminum, copper, iron, hibiscus acid protocatechuic acid, heterogeneous acid polysaccharides, phenolic compounds, flavonoids, β-carotene, riboflavin, thiamine, niacin, and the

ascorbic, malic and hibiscic acids.

Ethnomedical Uses	The dry calyx of this plant which is dark-red in colour when dried, possesses great commercial value because of its use as a plant colorant for food and drugs as well as beverage. It also being found to have antihypertensive properties (Haji-Faradi and HajiTarkhani, 1999). The plant is used to treat hypertension, pyrexia, inflammation, liver disorders, kidney and urinary bladder stones, and obesity (Liu et al., 2006). Its leaves are commonly used as a diuretic, sedative and refrigerant, and its fruits are considered to be an anti-scorbutic. Apart from having beverage properties, the calyces are used as diuretic, an intestinal anti-septic, a mild laxative, and aid in heart and nerve conditions to lower blood pressure and to treat calcified arteries (Ajay et al., 2007; Onyenekwe et al., 1999).
Precaution for use	Constant consumption in man may produce toxic effects (Alarcon-Aguilar, 2007). Results of histopathological studies on animals showed that prolonged usage of the extract in high quantity can cause liver injury while the effect was mild at small quantity. Though the average consumption of 150–180 mg/kg per day appears safe, the extracts should be taken with caution (Alarcon-

	Aguilar et al., 2007).
Dosage and Dosage form	Decoction "Zobo" is a popular drink among the native communities in West Africa with no specific dosage regime. Generally for decoction, 30 g of dried calyx should be considered for 900 ml of water and then boil until reduced to 600 ml. Then, 1 teaspoon should be taken three times a day..

21. Hymenocardia acida

Botanical Name	Hymenocardia acida
Common name	Heart-fruit (English), Cœurs-volants (French),
Local name	Burkina Faso: Dioula – Grengeni; komoni; tanyaro, Fulfuldé – samatahi;gnohi;péléti
	Ghana: Akan – Duakokowa, Brong – Sabrakyi

	Mali: Bambara – Grègnéni, Malinké – Diegbè, Pular – Pellitoro Senegal: Wolof – Enkélèn
Description	The plant is a small savanna tree or shrub of about 9 m high with branches which are rusty brown as the bark peels and form a fairly heavy, somewhat rounded crown. The bark is smooth or flaky and is pinkish-brown when fresh but turns into pale brown or grey eventually. Leaves are thin, leathery, elliptic-oblong which may grow up to 8.75 cm long and 3.75 cm wide. The leaves are usually pubescent when young with and have dense mat of fine hairs and with golden glands beneath. The apex is obtuse to rounded, the base is obtuse, the petiole is slender in shape, and is up to 1.8 cm long. Flowers are unisexual. The male flowers are reddish-yellow, occurring in clusters of spikes up to 6.5 cm long. Calyx is cupular, red, and the anthers are creamy white. The female flowers are green which are placed on axils of leafy lateral branches and bear a prominent stigma which spread about 1.25 cm. Fruit is compressed, obcordate and reddish-brown, and is about 2.5 cm long and 2.5-3.75 cm wide, developing in pairs along one edge, each of which with a thin pale brown nearly square wing. Seed are flattened, and are glossy brown in colour.

Habitat and Distribution	The plant is found in the Sudanese and Guinean savannas on a land that is a little bit sandy, loamy or clay. It is also present in savanna and deciduous woodlands, often on lakeside dunes and occurs in tropical Africa from Senegal to Cameroun.
Plant part of interest	Stem-bark, root-bark
Chemical constituents	Th chemicals that are available include sterols, proanthocyanidins, coumarins, flavonoids, triterpenoids (betulinic acid and lupeol) (Diallo, 2004); alkaloid (hymenocardine peptide) (Pai et al. 1968); tannins
Ethnomedical Uses	Decoction of the leaves is used to treat malaria (Vonthron-Senecheau et al., 2003), diabetes and skin ulcers (Igoli and Gray, 2008). The decoction of the roots is used as a mouthwash against caries and bad breath (Kerharo and Adam, 1974). It is hypotensive, antipyretic and antimalarial (Bernard, 2001) and also used to treat sickle cell crises (Mpiana et al. , 2007), stomatitis, diarrhoea, dysentery, gastric ulcers, colic and painful periods (Ukwe, 1997). When mixed with honey, the leaf decoction is used to treat digestive disorders (Ukwe, 1997). The infused mixture of bark and leaves is used against respiratory disorders, hypertension, epilepsy and insanity (Basilevskaia, 1969; Diallo,

	2002).
Precaution for use	Do not exceed the recommended doses
Dosage and Dosage form	Decoction: Boil about 90 g of leaves in 500 ml water for about 30 minutes. Take 1 cup (about 75 ml) 3 X per day (per-os)

22. Khaya senegalensis

Botanical Name	Khaya senegalensis
Common name	Mahogany of dry zone, mahogany, African cedar (English); Cailcedrat du Sénégal, Acajou du Senegal (French)
Local name	Burkina Faso: Mooré – kuka, Dioula – Djala, Fulfuldé – kayi;kayl Cote d'Ivoire: Malinké – Jala
	Ghana: Twi – Kuntunkuri, Fante – Okum, Ewé- Logo
	Mali: Bambara – Jala, Dogon – Pell,

	Peulh – Kaille
	Nigeria: Yoruba – Oganwo, Hausa – Madaci, Ibo – Ono onu Senegal: Serer - N'garin, Wolof – Hay, Diola – Bu ririt
	Togo: Ewé – Mahougen, Ouachi – Mahougani
Description	It is a tree that grows up to 40 m high with a width of about 4 m. it branches into 2-3 main limbs at about 8 m that gives it giving a wide spread crown. It has pinnately, compound leaves with 6-8 pairs of leaflets. The leaf shape is elliptic-lanceolate. And leaves are opposite and glabrous. Inflorescence contains flowers that are cream-coloured (Adegbola, 1986).
Habitat and Distribution	Widely distributed in the savanna forests of Africa
Plant part of interest	Stem bark
Chemical constituents	Limonoids (methyl angolensate, khayalenoids A and B), 2, 6-dihydroxybenzoquinone, capsterol, stigmasterol and β-sitosterol; scopoletin, scoparone and aeculetin (Yuan et al. 2009; Zhang et al., 2009).
Ethnomedical Uses	The stem bark is bitterwhich makes it usedful as a remedy for fever. The fresh bark is macerated in cold water or the dried bark is pulverized and

	mixed with salt is taken in small doses every other day to treat stomachic and bitter tonic, depurative, vermifuge and taenicide to treat syphilis. Cold infusion of the bark is given to horses as a tonic to improve appetite and to cattle suffering from liver fluke. Dried pulverized bark is used as a dressing for ulcers on the backs of camels and horses (Adesogan et al., 1967; Androulakis et al., 2006).
Precaution for use	It prepared medicine from this plant may interfere with the metabolism of some drugs in liver because of its antihepatoxic and hepatic detoxification properties. The ethanolic extract of Khaya senegalensis exerted more severe effect on the kidney when administered continuously over a prolonged period than a short one and this will adversely affect the functioning of the kidney (Adebayo et al., 2003).
Dosage and Dosage form	Decoction: 30 g of roasted ground seeds put in 900 ml water to simmer until it reduced to 600 ml. Then, 1 teacup should be taken three times daily Tincture: 1:5 in 50% alcohol 5 ml three times daily.

23. Lawsonia inermis

Botanical Name	Lawsonia inermis
Common name	Henna, Egyptian privet (English); Henné (French)
Local name	Burkina Faso: Mooré – Lalé, Dioula – Djabi, Fulfuldé – Djabe;Lêlla Ghana: Dagbani – Z abella, Hausa – Lalle
	Mali: Bambara – Dabé, Maninka-Dyabi, Pular – Dyabè, Sérère – Fuden
	Nigeria: Yoruba – Laali
	Senegal: Soussou – Laali, Wolof – Fuden, Malinké – Djabi
Description	This plant is a shrub that is highly branched and grows between 2 to 9 m tall. It possesses smooth, white and fibrous bark. Leaves are simple, opposite and entire, sessile to subsessile and pinnately veined. Inflorescence is a terminal panicle and pyramidal of 10 to 25 cm long. It has

	very fragrant bisexual, white and hairless flowers. Fruits are capsuloid balls of 8 mm in diameter and are glabrous, indehiscent and turn to light brown at maturity.
Habitat and Distribution	The plant is widely distributed around Iran, Pakistan and Western India. It is also found cultivated in home gardens and near houses in the Mediterranean, tropical, subtropical and Sahelian regions of Africa (Aweke et al., 2005).
Plant part of interest	Leaf
Chemical constituents	Quinones (lawsone and 2-hydroxy-1, lawsoniaside, 1,4naphthoquinone); xanthones (laxanthones); flavonoids (luteolin, luteolinglycosides, acacetine,); tannins; coumarins (lacoumarine, scopoletin, esculetin); naphthalene derivatives; sterols (β-sitosterol, stigmasterol, daucosterol); pentacyclic triterpenes (hennadiol, lupeol, betulin betulinic acid) and essential oils
Ethnomedical Uses	The infused leaves are used to treat trypanosomiasis (Aweke et al., 2005) and the leaf decoction is used against malaria (Loua, 2004).
Precaution for use	It is recommended that the liver function should constantly be checked during treatment
Dosage and	Infusion: 30 g dried leaves in 600 ml

Dosage form	of water. Then, 34 teacups should be taken daily.
	Tincture: 1:5 in 45% alcohol. 5 ml should be taken three times daily

24. Lippia multiflora

Botanical Name	Lippia multiflora
Common name	Bush tea; Gambian tea bush; Healer herb; Ti-tree English), Thé de Gambie (French).
Local name	Burkina Faso: Mooré – Kwilgwisaoré, Dioula – Kangaliba, Fulfuldé – Légal café
	Cote d'Ivoire: Anyi – Amaniena, Kalango – Akankoino, Maninka – Sonugba Suba
	Gambia: Fular–Usumbolomo, Mandika– Killiba (Sisilinghyamo), Wolof – Mbormbor

	Ghana: Akan – Sre-Nunum, Ga – Naasuruu, Ewe – Afudoti (Afu) Guinea: Fula Pulaar – Bahe, Susu – Diohuli
	Mali: Fula Pulaar – Bahe-Bahe, Manding Bambara – Gane Ba Nigeria: Fula Fulfulde – Dirisi, Yoruba – EfinrinGogara Fefe Senegal: Balanta – Brege, Serer – Mbalat, Diola – Busag
	Sierra Leone: Temne – A-Kimbo
	Togo: Tem – Fasau Klouto – Avudati, Ewe – Nyone
Description	This is a stout woody, aromatic perennial shrub that bears ridged stems. It has simple leaves that is characterised with oblong lanceolate shape, thick texture, dentate margin, lateral veins, and are bluish-green in colour. Flower is whitish and sweet-scented and the inflorescence is branched.
Habitat and Distribution	Guinea and coastal savannah and also in tropical West Africa
Plant part of interest	Leaf
Chemical constituents	Contains volatile oil (including linalool, camphor, terpineol, thymol and other monoterpenes), flavonoid, saponin (glycoside) (Pelissier, 1994;

	GHP, 1992).
Ethnomedical Uses	The plant is popularly used as an aromatic tea in African traditional medicine and other regions of the world. It leaves are used as a hot beverage and a tea-like infusion for fevers, gastrointestinal disturbances, coughs and colds. Rural communities in some parts of West Africa take Lippia tea after a hard day's work to relax and enhance sleep. While in urban areas the tea is taken in the morning to relieve stress. Infusion of the leaves is used for the treatment of malarial and microbial infections in Ghana and Nigeria (Kerharo and Adam, 1974; Kunle et al., 2003; Ajaiyeoba et al., 2004). The tea is also used traditionally as an antihypertensive, and a laxative. A drink made from the bolied leaves and palm nut is used to expel placenta after delivery (Burkill, 1997; Irvine, 1961). In Mali the powdered leaf is used in the production of a remedy for treating malaria (Diallo et al., 2004).
Precaution for use	Caution should be taken in the administration of the aqueous extract in patients with compromised liver and renal function especially at high doses
Dosage and Dosage form	Infusion; tincture; spray Infusion: 30 g dried leaves in 600 ml of water; 3-4 teacups daily Tincture: 1:5 in 45%

---

alcohol; 5 ml three times daily

---

25. Mitragyna inermis

Botanical Name	Mitragyna inermis
Common name	False abura (English)
Local name	Burkina Faso:Mooré – Yiilga, Dioula – Djum, Fulfildé – kwali;koli;kadiolé
	Ghana: Dagare – Ila, Akan – Kukyamfie
	Nigeria: Igbo – Akpatenyi Senegal: Arabic – Agbal
	Togo: Ewe – Lenkati, Mina – Elikpati, Moba – Yelowum
Description	A tree grows up to 16 m high high, often branches from the base and possesses erect stem, with rounded, open crown. Its bark is smooth to rough, grey to pale brown, with pale

	brown, fibrous slash. Stems are pubescent, pale brown. Leaves are opposite, glabrous or more or less pubescent beneath on nerves or finely pubescent, elliptic or obovate, pointed or shortly acuminate at apex, cuneate, rounded or subcordate at base. The young leaves are often red-tinged with leaf petiole of 0.6-1 cm long. Also, the leaves have pinnate nerves. Tertiary venation more or less visible. Inflorescence is solitary, compact, and has globose head, with a 3-9 cm long glabrous peduncle which may be terminal or at the base of a leaf, composing of a great number of fragrant flowers. The flowers are sessile, white or creamy coloured, with glabrous tubular calyx. The flowers are 5-lobed, has tubular corolla, and has bottle-brush shaped style. Inflorescence is spherical, brown, turns blackish, 1.2-1.8cm in diameter, persisting for a long time on the tree. Fruit is a small, oblong capsule, about 5 mm long, topped by a horny crown shape, dehiscing into two halves to reveal a great number of seeds
Habitat and Distribution	
Plant part of interest	
Chemical	Indole alkaloids (rhynchophylline,

constituents	rotundifoline, speciophylline and uncarine); tripterpenoid saponins (inermiside I and inermiside II) [Cheng et al., 2002; Shellard and Sarpong, 1969, 1970; Shellard et al., 1971)
Ethnomedical Uses	It is used in treatment of liver disease, stomach and intestinal disorders; malaria; hypertension (Adjanohoun et al., 1985; Phillipson and Wright, 1991), abortifacient, vermifuge; antiemetic, debility, analgesic and pain-killer.
Precaution for use	Caution should be taken in the administration of the aqueous extract in patients with an abnormal renal function and in heart disease especially at high doses
Dosage and Dosage form	Decoction: 30 g leaf per litre of water, boil for 10-15 minutes, take a cupful three times daily Tincture: 1-5 in 45% alcohol; 5 ml three times daily

26. Momordica charantia

Botanical Name	Momordica charantia
Common name	Balsam pear, African cucumber, Cundeamor, Bitter apple, Bitter melon, Carilla plant, Wild cucumber, Bitter cucumber (English); Poire de balsame, Concombre Africain, Margose, liane/pomme de merveilles (French).
Local name	Benin: Fon / Goun – Nyèsinkèn, Yorouba – Edjini, Dendi – Atakluma Burkina Faso: Fulfildé – Njalam fetuhi Côte d'Ivoire: Adioukrou – Sing Biep, Guéré- N'guéné Boué Ghana: Akan – Nyanya, Ewe – Kakle, Hausa – Daddagu Nigeria: Yoruba – Ejinrin Togo: Ewe – Agnagnran, Adja –

	Adounka, Mina – Guêssikan
Description	This is a climbing herbaceous, tendril-bearing vine that grows to 5 metres long. It bears digital, lobed, alternate, petiolate, long-stalked leaf that is provided with copetiolar tendrils fine and simple blade. It is generally pentagonal, and divided into five main lobes and is 2 to 6 cm long, 10 to 25 mm wide. It has a rounded top: 2-5 secondary veins per lobe. The leaf-base deeply cordate and 3-veined with hair soft and smooth on both sides, thin top, longer and denser on the veins beneath. The plant has golden yellow flowers of 3 cm wide, 5 lobes obtuse at the top corner, with three longitudinal ridges. The male flowers on top of an axillary peduncle is 4 to 7 cm long with leafy bracts cordate slightly above the base. While the female flowers are at the top of the ovary with peduncle of 3 to 4 cm and covered with dense spines. The fruit is berry, distinct warty exterior and oblong shape, hollow in cross-section, with a thin layer of flesh surrounding a central seed cavity filled with large flat seeds and pith. Its seeds and pith appear white in unripe fruits. It is bright orange at maturity, 3 to 6 cm long, 2-3 cm wide, with soft spines. As the fruit ripens, the flesh becomes tougher, bitterer and too distasteful.
Habitat and	The plant is a tropical plant species

Distribution	that is widely grown in Asia, Africa, and the Caribbean for its edible fruit. It is native to India, but widespread throughout the tropics, occurring as a weed along roadsides, in bushes or shrubs and abandoned crops and outskirts of town in areas with more or less humid climate. (GHP, 1992).
Plant part of interest	Leaf and fruit
Chemical constituents	Contains charantin, vicine, polypeptide-p, momordicine 1, 2 and 3, momorcrines A and B, momordine, arginine, aaspartic acid, leucine, leusine, tyrosine, fixed oil, acid resins, vitamin C, carotene, γ-aminobutyric acid, mineral salts (e.g. salts of silicon, calcium, phosphorus, strontium, copper, lead, zinc, sodium and iron), pectic acid, pectin, saponins, 5-hydroxytryptamine, albumin, globulin and glutelin rich in essential amino acids and vitamin B, carotene and alpha-amino butyric acids, alkaloids, saponins (Olaniyi and Marquis, 1975).
Ethnomedical Uses	Yorubas tribe of Nigeria use the decoction is used to treat malaria and in Senegal, the leaves are used for fever, whilst the fruits and leaves are used against itchy skin conditions like scabies (Paulino de Albuquerque et al., 2007). The decoction of the leaves is used to treat mouth sores, gangrenous wounds and gastric ulcers

	(Agyare et al., 2009), while the whole plant is used to treat malaria, stomach ache, stomach acidity, fever, diarrhoea, intestinal parasites and kidney complaints (Luziatelli et al., 2010). Fruit, tender shoots and tender roots are used for diabetes, blood purification and snake bite. Others also use the leaves to treat rabies, chest and rheumatic pains (Pradhan and Badola, 2008).
Precaution for use	Blood sugar level should be monitored of administration of aqueous leaf and bark extract. Avoid co-administration with other antidiabetic medicines except under medical supervision
Dosage and Dosage form	Decoction: 30 g dried aerial parts should be put in 900 ml water, simmer until reduced to 600 ml. Then, one teacup three times daily Infusion: 30 g dried aerial parts should be put in 600 ml of water. One teacup should be taken three times daily Tincture: 1:5 in 45% alcohol. 5 ml three times daily Capsules: 1-2 g of powdered leaf, 1 capsule two times daily

27. Morinda lucida

Botanical Name	Morinda lucida
Common name	Brimstone tree (English) Arbre à soufre, oruwo
Local name	Burkina Faso: Dioula – Mangana
	Ghana: Akan – Bronyadua Konkroma
	Nigeria: Igbo – Nuke, Yoruba – Oruwo
	Sierra Leone: Mende – Hojologbo
	Togo: Ewé – Dzadzaklan, Ouatchi – Dadaklan, Adja – Tsikémachou
Description	This is an evergreen shrub or small to medium-sized tree up to 18-25 metres tall, with bole and branches often crooked or gnarled. The bark is smooth to roughly scaly, grey to brown, often with some distinct purple layers. Leaves opposite, simple

---

and entire; stipules ovate or triangular which are 1-7 mm long, petiole up to 1.5 cm long. The leaf blade is elliptical, 6-18 cm × 2-9 cm, base rounded to cuneate, apex is acute to acuminate, shiny above, sometimes finely pubescent when young. Inflorescence a stalked head 4-7 mm in diameter, 1-3 at the nodes opposite a single leaf. The peduncle is up to 8 cm long bearing at base a stalked cupshaped gland. Flowers are bisexual, regular, 5merous, heterostylous, fragrant. Calyx is cupshaped of about 2 mm long and persistent. Corolla is salver-shaped and about 1.5 cm long and is white or greenish yellow in colour. Ovary is inferior, 2-celled, style 8-11 mm long with 2 stigma lobes 4-7 mm long. Stamens is 5. Fruit a drupe, several, together arranged into an almost globose succulent syncarp 1-2.5 cm in diameter, soft and black when mature. Seed si ellipsoid, about 3.5 mm × 2 mm × 0.5 mm, yellowish, soft.

Habitat and Distribution	Morinda lucida occurs from Senegal to Sudan and southward to Angola and Zambia. It is sometimes planted around villages and grows in grassland, exposed hillsides, thickest forests, often on termite mounds, sometimes in areas which are regularly flooded, from sea-level up to 1300 m altitude.

Plant part of interest	Leaf, root and stem bark
Chemical constituents	Anthraquinones (Durodola, 1974, Koumaglo et al., 1992; Sittie et al., 1999); urosilic acid and other triterpenoid acids (Cimanga et al., 2006; Adebayo and Kretti, 2011).
Ethnomedical Uses	M. lucida is an important plant in traditional medicine in West Africa,. Decoctions and infusions of roots, bark and leaves are recognized remedies for the treatment of different types of fever (including yellow fever), malaria, trypanosomiasis and bouts of fever during labour. The plant is also used in cases of diabetes, hypertension, stroke, dysentery, stomach pain, ulcers, leprosy and gonorrhoea. In Nigeria, M. lucida is one of the four most commonly used traditional remedies against fever. In Cote d'Ivoire, a bark decoction is used against jaundice, and in DR Congo it is combined with the powdered root bark as a poultice to treat the itch and ringworm The fruits are used in the treatment of asthma (Chin, 2002) While the infusion or decoction of the leaves and bark of the trunk, are used in the treatment of oral cancer (Ashida et al., 2010). The decoction of the bark of the trunk is also used in the treatment of haemorrhoids and gastric ulcer

	(Agyare et al., 2009).
Precaution for use	Caution should be taken in the administration of the aqueous extract in patients with compromised renal and liver functions
Dosage and Dosage form	Decoction: 30 g of the plant material placed in 900 ml water, simmer until reduced to 600 ml. 1 teacup three times daily

28. Moringa oleifera

Botanical Name	Moringa oleifera
Common name	Horse radish Tree; Drumstick Tree; Ben Oil Tree; Miracle Tree; Clarifier Tree; Kelor Tree; Mother's Best Friend, French; Mourongue; Moringa
Local name	Burkina Faso: Moore – Arzan Tiiga, Dioula – ArdjinaYiri, Fulfuldé – Gilgandja

Ghana: Dagari – Zangala, Ewe – Babatsi, Hausa – Zingaridende

Mali: Bambara – Nevrede, Mandigue – Nebedayo

Nigeria: Yuroba – Ewe Igbale, Hausa – Danga

Senegal: Wolof – Nebeday

Togo: Ewe – Yovovigbe, Ouatchi – Kpotsi, Lamba – Spe

Description   It is a small to medium sized perennial tropical tree which grows up to 12 m high at maturity and forms drooping branches. It has stem brittle with a corky bark. It has umbrella-shaped crown and usually has a single stem of soft wood and light bark. The tree develops caudexed base with age. Leaves are leathery, dark green on upper side and pale green or almost ashy on lower side. The compound or tri-pinnate leaf has up to nine leaflets (or pinnae) with wide variation in sizes that ranges about 0.7-5.3 cm long and 0.3-3.6 cm wide. Leaflets are petiolate (of 0.1-0.4 cm long), have entire margins, obtuse, rounded or emarginated apices with reticulate venation, oppositely arranged on primary, secondary and tertiary axes. The shapes of leaflets range from elliptic, ovate to obovate, terminal leaflets, obovate and larger than elliptically or ovately shaped lateral ones, leaflets quite pale when young, bases of leaflets symmetrical, acute, rounded or obtuse. Dry leaflets are feathery and papery in texture and brownish to yellowish green in colour. Inflorescences are axillary, shorter than leaves. Flowers are creamy coloured or white, 2.5 cm in diameter. Stamens are yellow, appear in panicles during periods of stress. Fruits or pods are pendulous, green and succulent when young and brown when mature, triangular, tapering at both ends. It can grow within the range of 30-120 cm long and 1.8 cm wide and splits lengthwise into 3 parts when it became dry. Each pod contains about 20 seeds and is dark brown with 3 papery wings.

Habitat and Distribution

M. oleifera is believed to be native to the sub-Himalayan tracts of Northern India. It grows in savanna tropics, probably spreading through intensive cultivation for various purposes. Moringa tree was introduced to Africa from India at the turn of the twentieth century (Muluvi et al., 1999). M. oleifera is more important in relatively more arid regions of west Africa. It is found in the northern regions of Ghana, in Mali and in more arid northern parts of Nigeria. Moringa is naturally found in Malawi, Niger, Senegal and Tanzania. In India, the

	young pods used as drumsticks are canned and exported all over the world. It grows well in the humid tropics' high heat, desiccating dryness or destitute soils. However, Moringa grows best on dry sandy soil and yields much less foliage when it is exposed to too much water. It can be grown as annual or greenhouse plant in temperate zones.
Plant part of interest	Leaves, fruits, seeds, bark and root.
Chemical constituents	Estrogenic substances (including β-sitosterol), pectinesterase; pterygospermin; alkaloids (moringine and moringinine), acetylated glycosides (e.g. niaziminin A, niaziminin B niazirin, niazirinin), (Faizi et al., 1995; Murakami et al., 1998), glycosides containing isothiocyanates (Faizi et al., 1994); (4-[(4'-Oacetyl (Evans, 1996); β-carotene, reducing sugars, tannins, flavonoids and cardiac glycosides (Evans, 1996); β-carotene, reducing sugars; tannins, flavonoids and cardiac glycosides
Ethnomedical Uses	The plant is cultivated for its leaves, fruits, roots and seeds for a variety of uses, both food and drug. Almost every part of the plant is valuable as food. However, the leaves and pods are more used as food sources or supplements. The young leaves of M.

oleifera are edible and are part of the traditional diets in many countries where the tree grows and are eaten cooked or added to food as dried leaf powder. The seeds are eaten as peanuts and the oil from it is edible. Thickened roots are used as substitute for horseradish. One most notable use of Moringa leaf powder is for the treatment and prevention of malnutrition, especially in children. The record of medicinal uses of M. oleifera in folklore is abundant. Plant parts other than the leaves are responsible for most of the medicinal uses of the plant, especially the roots and seeds. However, the leaves also have medicinal uses in folklore. Flowers, leaves and roots of the plant are used for tumours. The leaves as poultice, is applied to sores or rubbed on the temples as a treatment for headaches. The poultice of leaves is also used in reducing glandular swellings. The leaves are used as a purgative, to promote digestion and in traditional medicine as a hypocholesterolemic agent in obese individuals. The juice extracted from the leaves is applied directly on to the eye for the treatment of conjunctivitis. It is also warmed and applied to affected areas to relieve the pain associated with sprain. The leaves are used in a preparation which is cooked and taken for the treatment of high

	blood pressure. In India, the plant is used as an abortifacient (Nath et al., 1992
Precaution for use	Caution should be taken in the administration of the aqueous extract in patients with compromised renal and liver functions.
Dosage and Dosage form	Powder, decoction, tincture The leaf is eaten as a leafy vegetable either raw or boiled. For decoction boil 30 g of the dried leaves in 900 ml water; simmer until reduced to 600 ml; 1 teacup three times daily

29. Ocimum basilicum

Botanical Name	Ocimum basilicum
Common name	English: Sweet Basil French: Basilic, Basilic aux sauces, Basilic commun, Basilic romain, Framboisin (Antilles), Herbe Royale, Oranger Savetiers, Des

	Pistou
Local name	Burkina Faso: Mooré – Yulin-gnuuga, Dioula – chou kolan, Fulfuldé – Ngunguné;gugumã
	Cote d'Ivoire: Baule – Emia
	Ghana: Akan – Nunum, Ga – Sulu, Ewe – Dzevetu
	Mali: Bambara – Chou Kolan
	Nigeria: Yoruba – efinrin wewe
	Sierra Leone: Kono – Peinga
	Togo: Akasalem – Kunyonyo
Description	This is a small, annual aromatic herb, like a-shrub. Its stems are quadrangular, branched and forming compact balls of light green color. serrated leaves, clearly stalked, thin, elliptical, ovate or oblong cuneate at the base and acuminate at apex. It grows from 2 to 4 cm long. It has a whorled inflorescence up to 20 cm with very short pedicels. The inflorescence is curved, loose terminal racemes of white flowers, has white petals measuring 4-5 mm, calyx lobes orbicular to higher than 6 mm in diameter, limb 2-lipped, upper lip is 3toothed, middle tooth is circular to obovate, margin winged, decurrent, lateral teeth is shorter; lower lip has 2 toothed , teeth narrower, apex is

	acuminate to spinescent, sometimes approximate. The corolla tube is slightly shorter than calyx or rarely exserted, dilated, obliquely campanulate at throat. Limb 2lipped, upper lip sub-equally (3- or 4 -lobed), lower lip is somewhat elongated or not, declined. The margin is entire, flat or slightly concave. It has 4 stamens, exerted, declined on lower corolla lip, anterior[y 2 are longer. Filaments are free or anterior 2 connate at base. Anthers are ovoid-reniform, 1-locellate. Style is longer than stamens with 2-cleft at apex.
Habitat and Distribution	The plant grows well in sandy and loamy well-drained soils, but it prefers acidic, neutral and basic (alkaline) soils. It cannot grow in the shade and requires moist soil, preferably on cultivated beds.
Plant part of interest	Leaf
Chemical constituents	Contains essential oils such as linalool, epi-α-cadinol, αbergamotene, γ-cadinene, eugenol, chavicol, anethole, estragole, limonene, cuminaldehyde, α-terpineol and cinamic acid derivatives (Abdulah et al., 2008; Politeo, 2007)
Ethnomedical Uses	Sweet basil has been used for many years as a culinary as well as medicinal herb. It plays an important

role in the digestive and nervous systems, easing flatulence, stomach cramps and indigestion. The leaves and top of the flower are antispasmodic, aromatic, carminative, digestive, galactogogue, stomachic and tonic (Singh et al., 2011). It is used in the treatment of feverish illnesses like colds and influenza. It is also used to treat poor digestion, nausea, and abdominal cramps, gastro-enteritis, migraine, insomnia, depression and exhaustion. It is alsp applicable in cases of acne, loss of smell, insect stings, snake bites and skin infections. The leaves can be harvested throughout the growing season and are used fresh or dried (Njorege, 2006). The seed is having mucilage and is taken as an infusion in the treatment of gonorrhoea, dysentery and chronic diarrhoea, and is also claimed to remove film and opacity from the eyes. The root is used in the treatment of bowel complaints in children. Extracts from the plant are bactericidal and anti-parasitic. In India, sweet basil is used for dental ailments due to its proposed antimicrobial effects (Patel and venkatakrishna, 1988).

Precaution for use	Care should be taken in patients with hypoglycaemia and liver problem. Basil oil contains estragole a potentially carcinogenic and

	mutagenic agent. It should not be taken during pregnancy or given to small infants/children
Dosage and Dosage form	Decoction: 30 g plant material is placed in 900 ml water; simmer until it reduced to 600 ml. Then, 1 tablespoonful is taken two times daily

30. Ocimum gratissimum

Botanical Name	Ocimum gratissimum
Common name	Tea Bush, mosquito plant, fever leaf, fever plant of Sierra Leone, French: Basilic de ceylan
Local name	Cote d'Ivoire: Anyi – Samane, Baule – Aloamagneree, Fulfulde – Cunfere Ghana: Adangme – Gbekona, Akan – Onunum , Ga – Sru Sulu Suru Guinea Bissau: Crioulo – Doreda Guinea: Manding Maninka – Su-Guen-Fira Nigeria: Edo – Aramogho, Hausa –

	Dai Dooyaata Gidaa, Igbo – Ncho-Anwu Nchuagwunta, Yoruba-efinrin nla Senegal: Crioulo – Doreda, Fula – Kunfere, Maninka – Sukuru Baba, 'Susu' Barikiri Togo: Ewe – Dzogbeti, Akaselem – Ditsunonon
Description	The plant is an erect shrub that grows up to a height of 1.8 m; the stems are nearly glabrous with leaves, which have rather long petiole, lanceolate to oblong-lanceolate or ovate or obovate, cuneate or asymmetric base, apex acute or acuminate, margin toothed or distantly serrated, up to 12 cm long, 4 cm broad; flowers are cream-white or yellowish, pedicel puberulous, calyx two-lipped, upper lip ovate, lower lip oblong, two-teethed; occurring in paniculate racemes usually 15 cm long with green colour at the bud stage but turns brown when dry (Trease and Evans, 1972).
Habitat and Distribution	It is widely distributed in the tropics including Africa and can be found mainly in gardens, compounds, old farms near villages, and is often cultivated in various parts of West Africa. It is found across many parts of Nigeria, both north and south.
Plant part of interest	Leaf
Chemical	Volatile oil (e.g. thymol, eugenol, alpha and βpinene, camphene,

constituents	terpinene, limonene and methyl eugenol; camphor, caryophylline); triterpenes; reducing sugars (GHP, 1992; Onajobi, 1986; Sainsbury and Sofowora, 1971; El Said et al., 1969).
Ethnomedical Uses	O. gratissimum is used in the treatment of upper respiratory tract (e.g pneumonia, etc.) and digestive problems (e.g. diarrhoea, dysentery), skin diseases, fever, headaches and conjunctivitis (Onajobi, 1986; Oliver-Bever, 1960). It is used in the treatment of malaria and small pox (Irvine, 1961). The leaves are used to treat nose bleeding and dizziness, and it is chewed with salt or boiled with it and used as febrifuge and diaphoretic. Fluid obtained when the leaf is squeezed in little water is used as an eye drop for ophthalmic conditions such as conjunctivitis. The leaf infusion is mixed with pepper to treat dysentery (Dalziel, 1936). Oil from the leaves is used to prevent mosquito bites and repel other insects. The leaves are also used to treat constipation, menorrhagia and abdominal colic. The whole plant is used for rheumatism and the root for snakebite (Adjanohoun et al., 1991).
Precaution for use	Caution should be taken in patients with hypoglycaemia and liver disorders. It may not be used in chronic constipation; its use in bleeding situations must be medically

supervised. Overdose or prolonged use may cause acute constipation and colonic inertial. It may also irritate mucous membranes when used externally in high doses; pregnancy and lactation.

Dosage and Dosage form

Essential oil Decoction: 30 g dried leaves placed in 900 ml water, simmer until reduced to 600 ml. 1 teacup should be taken three times daily Infusion: 30g of dried herb is placed in 600 ml of water. 1 teacupful should be taken three times a day Tincture: 1:5 should be placed in 50% alcohol, then 5 ml should be taken three times daily Essential oil: 2-3 drops should be taken three times daily

31. Phyllanthus niruri

Botanical Name	Phyllanthus niruri
Common name	Stone breaker, carry-me-seed, Creole senna, cane peas senna, quinine weed, hurricane weed, gale-wind weed, French: Herbe au chagrin
Local name	Burkina Faso: Mooré – Tinguin garga, Fulfuldé – Lébèl Cote d'Ivoire: Baules – Ugniassi, Kru Guere – Tienwe, Kulango – Lumbodiataka. Ghana: Twi – Bowomma guwakyi, Ga Dangme – Mbatoatshi, Nzema – Nwamenle Guinea Bissau: Fula Pulaar – Bubunguel Guinea: Kissi – Fundelo Un'do, Koranko – Kode, Toma – Sakade Nigeria: Edo – Orosorsor, Igbo – Ososo, Igbo (Ibuzo) – Awueli Sierra Leone: Mende – Eroboe
Description	This is an annual herb of around 30-50 cm high with grooved stem and slightly winged. Its leaves are simple, alternate and distichous, oblong-elliptical rounded at both ends. The leaves are pale green, 6-14 mm long and 25-5.5 mm broad. The flowers are unisexual, solitary with six sepals. The males part is in the lower axils and the females in the upper axils with deep dentate discs and very short

	styles. The fruit formed is capsule of about 2 mm in diameter.
Habitat and Distribution	Occurs commonly in gardens, dirty places and roadsides
Plant part of interest	Leaf
Chemical constituents	Alkaloids (securinine and related alkaloids), lignans (e.g. phyllanthin and hypophyllanthin), tannins, flavonoids (e.g. quercetin, rutin), methyl salicylate, carboxylic acid and saponins.
Ethnomedical Uses	Spanish called the plant as 'chanca piedra', which means "stone breaker" considering its folkloric use by Amazonians for eliminating gallstones and kidney stones. It is also used to treat hepatitis, colds, flu, fever, tuberculosis, malaria, diabetes, hypertension and liver diseases among others. In the Asian, Mediterranean regions and parts of east Africa, the plant is used as tea. Hot water extract of dried aerial parts administered orally is used as a diuretic and antimalarial (Weninger et al., 1986; Kitisin, 1952). The hot water extract of the fresh plant is also taken orally for gonorrhoea and other genitourinary diseases (Sahu, 1984; Khan et al., 1978). A decoction of the dried plant is used to cure coughs in infants and the fresh root is used to

cure jaundice. Infusion of young shoots is given to treat dysentery, and the leaves are commonly used to treat fever. It can also be used to increase appetite, relieve inflammations and as a remedy for anorexia (Asprey and Thornton, 1955). In India, the fruit is used for tubercular ulcers, scabies and ringworm. In the Fiji Islands, the dried planr that is grinded into powder is mixed with buttermilk is taken orally for jaundice. Fresh leaf juice is used to treat cuts and with castor oil and applied to the eye. Infusion of the green root is taken orally to treat heavy menstrual periods (Singh, 1986).

Precaution for use	Sugar levels and blood pressure to be checked during long-term treatment
Dosage and Dosage form	Liquid extract Decoction: 30 g dried leafy tops is placed in 900 ml water, simmer until it reduced to 600 ml. 1-3 cups should be taken daily
	Infusion: 30 g dried leaves is placed in 600 ml of water. 13 cups should be taken daily
	Tincture- 1:5 is placed in 50% alcohol, 5 ml should be taken three times daily. Fluid extracts/water-glycerine extracts: 1:1 is placed in 50% alcohol and 2-6 ml should be taken 2-3 times daily

32. Phytolacca dodecandra

Botanical Name	Phytolacca dodecandra
Common name	Endod, soap berry, African soap berry (English). Phytolaque, endod. Fitolaca (French)
Local name	Ghana: Akan – Ahoro Nigeria: Igbo – Ogwashi Okomofo Uburuku Aweli, Yoruba – Ososo
Description	This is a climbing' dioecious, semi-succulent shrub, with stems up to 10-20 m long and has a taproot. The trunk is sometimes up to 35 cm in diameter. The stems is usually glabrous. Leaves are alternate, simple and entire. Petiole is 1–4 cm long. Inflorescence is an axillary or terminal raceme of 5–30 cm long with many flowers, axis of the flower is hairy, the bracts is up to 2.5 mm long, shortly hairy, flowers functionally unisexual. The flower is

sweet-scented, pedicel is 2–8 mm long. The male flowers with narrowly oblong, about 2.5 mm long, reflexed, whitish to yellowish green sepals, petals is absent, stamens is 10-20 in 2 whorls, free, filaments 3-7 mm long, ovary usually rudimentary. Female flowers with oblong to ovate, about 2.5 mm long, reflexed sepals, accrescent in fruit, turning yellow to red, petals absent, stamens is 8-12, rudimentary, ovary is superior, consisting of 4-5 free, carpels is ovoid, styles is 1-2 mm long, curved, stigmas is linear; fruit consists of 4-5 1-seeded berries fused at base, up to 15 mm in diameter, fleshy, remains of style pointing outwards at apex, ripening orange or purplish red. Seeds is kidney-shaped and laterally is flattened, 2-4 mm long and is shiny black.

Habitat and Distribution	The plant is native to Sub-Saharan Africa and Madagascar and is introduced into Asia and tropical America. It is found in forest, forest margins, riparian forest, wet bushland, in fences along cultivated land and around houses, on mountain slopes and also in open fields, mostly at 1500–3000 m altitude. It grows best under direct sunlight in humid, slightly acidic soils that contain high levels of organic matter, in areas with an annual rainfall of about 1400 mm

	and a distinct dry period.
Plant part of interest	Fruit
Chemical constituents	Saponins (triterpenoid glycosides, aglycones of the glycosides are mainly composed of oleanolic acid, bayogenin , hederogenin and 2hydroxyoleanolic acid), phytosterols, lipids (palmitic acid, oleic acid, stearic acid); sugars, starches, pectins and gums (Parkhurst et al., 1973; Lemma et al., 19
Ethnomedical Uses	It is used in making traditional soap in Ethiopia, the plant berries are commonly used for washing and ridding clothes of lice and in control of fresh water snails (Pankhurst, 1965). It is also used for purging endo-parasites, for abortion, and against dandruff, gonorrhoea, ringworm, skin itching and other skin diseases (Watt and Breyer-Brandwijk, 1962, Esser et al., 2003). An extract of the roots, leaves, fruits and seeds of the plant is taken as a purgative, laxative, diuretic in Central and East Africa and Madagascar. These plant parts are used to treat a many diseases including worm infestations, oedema, diarrhoea, abdominal pain, wounds, scabies, eczema, psoriasis, leprosy, boils and vitiligo. An infusion of the fruit or the root decoction is widely taken to treat venereal diseases,

	bilharzia, rabies, malaria, sore throat and other respiratory problems, rheumatic pain and jaundice. In the East Africa ground leaves are applied to ^{tumours}, the root decoction is also drunk to cause vomiting as treatment of enlarged glands. In Tanzania macerated leaves or root bark are used to treat epilepsy while in Madagascar, a decoction of the aerial parts is applied to treat haemorrhoids. .
Precaution for use	The plant can be toxic and should be used with care
Dosage and Dosage form	Decoction: 30 g of dried plant material is placed in 900 ml water, simmer until reduced to 600 ml. 1-3 table-spoonfuls is taken daily

33. Pterocarpus erinaceus

Botanical Name	Pterocarpus erinaceus
Common name	English: African rosewood, Senegal rosewood, African barwood, African teak, African kino tree. French: Santal rouge d'Afrique, Vène, ven, palissandre du Sénégal, santal rouge d'Afrique, Portuguese: Pau sangue
Local name	Burkina Faso: Mooré – Noèèga ou Nohinga, Dioula – Gôni;gweni;mbeny, Fulfuldé – Bani ;banu ;bané ;bari
	Guinea: Maninka- Gbene – Gbin, Pular – Barybani Banigue, Kissi – Koilo Kouelo
	Mali: Bambara – Mguèni
	Nigeria: Hausa – Dorowan Kurmi, Igbo – Aze Egu, Yuroba – Apepe Senegal: Sérère – Ban, Wolof – Vèn,

	Malinké – N'gbéhun
Description	It is a small tree, with open rounded crown reaching about 15 to 20 m high, bole straight, cylindrical and devoid of branches to a height up to 10 m with light ribbed buttresses. The bark is brown, greyish to blackish, fissured and scaly; leaves alternate, odd-pinnate compound, with 5-11 leaflets. Inflorescence is axillary or terminal, paniculate, densely covered with brown hairs, bisexual flowers, with hairy pedicel, fruit pod circular, flattened and indehiscent.
Habitat and Distribution	The plant is found in the Sudano-Guinean on all types of soil including laterite
Plant part of interest	Leaf and stem bark
Chemical constituents	The plant contains homopterocarpine, angolensine, acetyloleanolic acid, pseudobaptigenine, alkaloids, tannins, saponins and flavonoids (Nuhu et al., 2000; Bevan et al., 1966; Akisanya et al., 1959).
Ethnomedical Uses	The plant is utilized in the treatment of fevers and sores. The infused leaf is used to treat diarrhoea, dysentery, and intestinal worms (Karou et al., 2003). The decoction or infusion of stem bark and roots is effective against bronchial infections, toothache, dysentery,

	painful menstruation, gonorrhoea, postpartum haemorrhage, tapeworm, leprosy, tumours and ulcers (Karou et al., 2003). The leaf decoction has aphrodisiac effect. It used as an insect repellent and to treat syphilis (Karou et al., 2003). The plant is also used against insomnia and skin fungal infections (Olowokudejo et al., 2008).
Precaution for use	Do not used more than recommended dosage
Dosage and Dosage form	300 g of plant material is boiled with 900 ml of water until it is reduced to 600 ml. Two table spoonfuls is taken twice daily.

34. Rauwolfia vomitoria

Botanical Name	Rauwolfia vomitoria
Common name	Swizzlestick, African Rauwolfia (English), Rauwolfia émétique

	(French).
Local name	Burkina Faso: Dioula – Kolidjohkhi, Fulfuldé – Moyatjalal;Ligéré Ghana: Akan – Kakapenpen; Ewe – Dodemak Powoe; Hausa – Wada Mali: Bambara – Kolijoi
	Nigeria: Yoruba – Asofeiyeje
	Togo: Ewe – Ou Adja, Dodemakpowoe; Akposso – Ilonotchi, Oklubètè;
	Senegal: Diola – Gi Upa
Description	The plant is a shrub or small tree that may grow up to 15 m high, with dichotomous branching. The leaves are whorled in groups of 4 or 5, variable, ovate shape, elliptic or oblong, acuminate apex, cuneate base, glabrous, lateral veins of 10-16 pairs; terminal inflorescence; flowered corymbs; small white flowers, 3-4 at node, numerous; fruit green, red when ripe (GHP, 2007).
Habitat and Distribution	The plant occurs naturally in gallery forests. It is native to Cameroon, Democratic Republic of Congo, Ghana, Liberia, Nigeria, Senegal, Sudan and Uganda, but now cultivated in many tropical and subtropical countries.
Plant part of	Root

interest	
Chemical constituents	Contains alkaloids (reserpine, serpentine, reserpoxidine, seredine, ajmaline, alstonine, isoajmaline, isoreserpiline, serpagine, raumatorine, rauvomitine, vomalidine, yohimbine, tetraphylline) and flavonoids (African pharmacopoeia 1985; Iwu and 1982; Paris, 1943; Amer and Court, 1980; Iwu and Court, 1982).
Ethnomedical Uses	The decoction of the leaves or roots is administered orally to treat mental illness (Iwu, 1993; Costa-Campos et al., 2004). The macerated leaf is used for the treatment of hypertension and fever, and the decoction is used against gonorrhoea, rheumatism, stunted growth, liver diseases, chronic skin diseases and skin parasites (Mesia et al., 2008). A root decoction is used to treat haemorrhoids (Agyare et al., 2009).
Precaution for use	The recommended dose should not be exceeded as this may provoke cholinergic symptoms and renal damage.
Dosage and Dosage form	Decoction: 30 g of dried sliced and chopped the roots and rhizome is placed in 900 ml water, simmer until is reduced to 600 ml. 1-3 cups should be taken daily (GHP, 2007) Tincture- 1:5 in 50% alcohol, 5 ml

should be taken three times daily

35. Sarcocephalus latifolius

Botanical Name	Sarcocephalus latifolius
Common name	African peach; Guinea peach; Country fig; Negro peach
Local name	Burkina Faso: Dagaari – Anguma, Fulfulde – Bakulehi, Grusi – Dianlo
	Cote d'Ivoire: Adyukru – Edik, Akye – Esubo Monleuh Sibo, Anyi – Balimbe Sibo Tere Gambia: Fula – Dundake, Mandinka – Bakaba, Ba-Tio, Wolof – Koba Nandok
	Ghana: Adangme – Akabi, Akan – Awintin, Dagbani – Galungun Guinea Bissau: Balanta – Cunhe Tetugole, Bioyogo – Canhame, Crioulo – Diunk Mali: Dogon – Ayugu, Manding Bambara – Bari Nigeria: Edo –

Aragbaihi, Hausa – Igiyaa Tafaashiyaa, Igbo – Mbiliinu, Yoruba – Egbesi Senegal: Vulgar – Dundake, Balanta – Batio Feas, Diola Flup – Bundufe

Sierra Leone: Bulom – Gbilgbil-Le, Fula – Dunduke, Gola – Yumbuyamba

Togo: Bassari – Degangande, Ewe – Alo Kubasa Kaio, Konkomba – Bunangim

Description	This is a strangling shrub or a small evergreen tree that grows up to 9 m in the savanna woodland. It has a rough bark. Leaves are elliptic or rounded-ovate, cuneate, with rounded or subcordate base and can be 10-20 cm long, 6-12 cm broad, glabrous, obovate, apex shortly and abruptly acuminate, upper surface darker, petiole red, stipules short, broad, ovate, and more persistent. Flowers on the pedicel are 1-2 cm long, flowerheads are white and is up to 5 cm in diameter, fragrantly sweet scented, sought by bees, becoming large and fleshy, not are drying hard, form reddish fleshy fruit that is comparatively shallow-pitted and grow up to 9 cm in diameter. Its fruiting season is between May-June and Sept.-Oct. Fruit is edible, sweetly acid pulp with numerous seeds embedded.

Habitat and Distribution	Common in the guinea savannah and also occurs in grassland savanna.
Plant part of interest	Root
Chemical constituents	The plant contains tannins, phenols, saponins, terpenes, steroids, reducing sugars, glycoalkaloids and indoloquinolizidine alkaloids (e.g. naucletine); carbohydrates, resins; bitter principles (GHP, 1992; Oliver-Bever, 1960), nauclefoline, and nauclechine (Hotellier et al., 1981).
Ethnomedical Uses	Extracts from the bark, root and leaves are used by natives of Africa for various ailments including sores, gonorrhoea, stomach disorder, cough and fever. The plant is used in Nigerian folk medicine in the treatment of piles and dysentery. An infusion of the bark has been widely used as a tonic and febrifuge, hence the description "African quinine" (Oliver-Bever, 1986). The pulverized root and bark have been used to treat sores and gonorrhoea in Sudan, Ghana, Ivory Coast and Nigeria (Irvine, 1961). Similarly, a decoction of the root bark is commonly employed in the treatment of stomach disorders, cough and malaria fever (Irvine, 1961). The herb has also been reported to be used as a component of arrow poison in Northern Nigeria and

	Cote d'Ivoire.
Precaution for use	Do not exceed the recommended doses
Dosage and Dosage form	Decoction: 250 g is macerated in about 600 ml "gin" (local alcoholic beverage) or hot water. 100 ml is taken orally two or three times a day depending on the severity of the feverish condition Tincture: 1:5 is placed in 50% alcohol, and 5 ml is takenS three times daily.

36. Sclerocarya birrea

Botanical Name	Sclerocarya birrea
Common name	Marula, Cider tree (English); Prunier d'Afrique, Sclérocarya à bière, prunier jaune, Poupartia (French).
Local name	Burkina Faso: Mooré – Nobéga;Noabga, Dioula–

N'gouna;kunan;kuntan, Fulfuldé – Hedi

Cote d'Ivoire: Malinké – N'guma

Ghana: Dagbani – M umuga, Mole – Noagba

Mali: Bambara – N'gunan Kutan 'Dao, Dogon – Bi, Peulh: He 'Di, Kedέ, 'Eri, Hέdέhi

Niger: Haussa–Dania, Zarma–Diney, Béribéri– Koma

Senegal: Wolof – Bir Ber, Basari – Ngudy

Description | The plant is a medium an erect, sized, single stemmed, terrestrial, perennial deciduous tree of about 10 to15 m in height. The stem-bark is flaky, with a grey mottled appearance due to contrasting grey and pale-brown pattern. Its leaves are composite, deciduous, imparipinnate, and range between 7 to 10 pairs of ovate, elliptical and glabrous leaflets. The leaflets are green above, lighter below and is usually only serrated when it is young, otherwise entire; flowers are small, dioecious, greenish, in spikes shorter than 2 cm long which are borne on small oblong clusters at the end of branches and usually appear before the leaves. The fruit is a green drupe on tree, falling off in autumn and turning light yellow on the ground. There are

	three seeds contained in the hard kernel, the fleshy pulp is highly nutritious. The female S. birrea trees bear plum-like stony fruits of about 30 mm in diameter (Ojewole, 2003).
Habitat and Distribution	The plant is native to tropical Africa and is widespread in Sudan-Sahel zone from Ethiopia in the North to Kwazulu-Natal (South Africa) in the south, also from Gambia in the west across to Nigeria and Cameroon in Central Africa and to Kenya and Sudan in the East (Belemtougri et al.,2007).The plant grows naturally in various types of woodland, on sandy soil or occasionally sandy loam.
Plant part of interest	Leaf, stem bark
Chemical constituents	Tannins (epicatechin-3-galloyl ester) is contained in the plant. Other constituents include alkaloids, saponins, flavonoids, terpenes, coumarins, triterpenoids, phytosterols, carbohydrates, oils, proteins, fibre, ascorbic acid and minerals (Ojewole et al., 2010; Bracca et al., 2003; Haidara, 1999; Smith et al., 1996; Galvez et al., 1992; Eromosele et al., 1991; Dao, 1988; Laurens, 1976; Kerharo and Adams, 1974).
Ethnomedical Uses	Sclerocarya birrea leaves are used to treat jaundice and the bark when combined with the leaves of

Cymbopogon gigentus, is used to treat ascites. The plant is also effective in the treatment of measles. A drink made from leaves is used for the treatment of gonorrhoea. Maceration of the stem bark is used in the treatment of abdominal pain, nausea, vomiting, syphilis, dysentery, rheumatism and has a prophylactic effect against malaria. The stem bark in combination with Momordica balsamina is indicated for snake bite or scorpion stings. The bark is an effective remedy for treating haemorrhoids. Pellets made from the bark are used for neuralgia in dental caries (Adjanohoun et al., 1980). In Ghana, the leaves are used to treat snakebite, and pruritus (filarial); the stem bark, the root and the fruits are used to treat pharyngitis, splenomegaly and goitre, respectively (Mshana et al., 2000). Externally, the paste of the bark is added to shear butter and applied to the forehead to treat migraine and blepharitis. The fruit juice is effective in the treatment of ear infections, constipation, hypertension, anorexia, and scurvy. The seeds are recommended by some therapists for asthenia (Kerharo and Adams, 1974).

Precaution for use	Aqueous extract of the plant can cause hypoglyacemia and increase hepatic and renal parameters. Monitor blood glucose biochemical parameters of the

<table>
<tr><td></td><td>liver and kidney regularly on prolonged use. Do not combine with other hypoglycaemic drugs except under specialist supervision.</td></tr>
<tr><td>Dosage and Dosage form</td><td>Preparation: 60g of dried leaves is placed in a pint of water and boil for 15 minutes and filter. Method of administration in the form of decoction orally Dosage according to blood sugar: Up to 2 g / l: 60 g is placed in 3 doses. Beyond 2 g / l: 100g in 3 doses and the treatment lasts 7 days. Maintenance therapy is done with a dose of 40 g in 2 doses.

Decoction: 30 g of ground seeds is placed in 900 ml of water and simmer until reduced to 600 ml, and drink a glass of water three times a day.

Tincture: 1:5 in 50% alcohol 5 ml three times daily</td></tr>
</table>

38. Scoparia dulcis

Botanical Name	Scoparia dulcis
Common name	English: Sweet broom; bitter broom; broom weed; licorice weed
Local name	Burkina Faso: Mooré – koostiiga, Dioula – N'timintiminin
	Ghana: Twi – Onyame ko metiri; Fante – Oguan nkyene, Ga – Shuoblo
	Mali: Bamabara – Ntimitimini, Bruturut
	Senegal: Balanta – Brutulut
	Sierra Leone: Bulom – Tjunkae
Description	This is an erect shrubby plant that grows to 20-70 cm high. Its stems are glabrous. Leaves are opposite or whorled, narrowly lanceolate, crenulate in upper half, narrowed, entire in lower half. Flowers are in

	slender racemes in upper leaf-axils, petals are four, white or bluish, bearded inside; fruit globose, capsule.
Habitat and Distribution	It is a common weed that is found in waste places in villages and on road and path sides as well as in marshy places. It is widely distributed in many tropical countries.
Plant part of interest	Leaf
Chemical constituents	Diterpenoids (scopadulcic acid A, B and C, scoparic acid A and scopadulin), scopadiol, scopadulciol, amellin, coumarins, saponins, tannins, amino acids, flavonoids (8hydroxytricetin-7-glucoronide, apigenin), alkaloids (6-methoxy benzoxazolinone), oleoresins, reducing sugars (Akendengue et al., 2005; Hayashi 2000; Nath, 1945).
Ethnomedical Uses	Scroparia dulcis is used in the treatment of diabetes, hypertension, abdominal problems, fever, inflammation, bronchitis, haemorrhoids and hepatosis (Hayashi, 2000; Satyanarayana 1969 Freire et al., 1993; Hayashi et al., 1993; Chow et al., 1974). The plant is used to treat burns, herpes, pimples, dysentery and hair loss (Luziatelli et al., 2010). Leaves of S. dulcis are used for dermatological (Rodrigues, 2006) and prostate disorders (Lans, 2007b). The

	whole plant is used in magico-religious rituals (Paulino de Albuquerque et al., 2007).
Precaution for use	Care should be taken in the administration of the aqueous extract in liver disease
Dosage and Dosage form	Infusion/decoction: 30 g is placed in 600 ml of water. 1 teacup is taken twice daily Tincture: 1:5 is placed in 60% alcohol, 5 ml is taken three times daily Capsules: 2-3 g twice daily

39. Securidaca longepedunculata

Botanical Name	Securidaca longepedunculata
Common name	Violet tree (English), Arbuste à Serpent (French)
Local name	Burkina Faso: Mooré – Palgu ;Pélga, Bissa – Hensasi, Dioula –

Djoro;Djoto, Fulfuldé – Alali

Cote d'Ivoire: Lobi – Samuele, Gagou: Dioro, Malinké – Diulo, Ndjuru Gambia: Malinké – Juto Djuto, Wolof – Fuf, Fula –Alali Ghana: Akan – Ofodo Kyrito Guinea Conakry: Malinké – Diodo, Fula – Diantu

Mali: Bambara – Djoro Dioro, Peulh – Iguili, Dogon – Toroe

Niger: Hausa – Warnagunguna, Fula – Adali, Djerma – Hasukore Nigeria: Hausa – Sanya, Fula: Adali, Adehi, Yoruba – Ipeta

Senegal: Diola – Fu Daray, Serer – Kuf Kuf, Wolof – Fuf

Togo: Ouatchi – Etritou, Mina – Metritu, Ewé – Kpeta

Sierra Leone: Malinké – Juto, Jodoo

Description The plant is semi-deciduous shrub or small tree that can grows to 12 m high, and often has flattened bole. It is much branched, and has an open or straggly looking crown. The young branches look drooping and pubescent. It has a bark smooth, thick and light yellow in nature and covers a yellow wood fibre. It has very thick roots and odour of methyl salicylate. The leaves are alternate, entire, simple, oblong-elliptic leaves and are

	5 to 6 cm long and 13-20 mm wide. It has a very fine hairs when it is young but losing these at maturity. The apex of the plant is rounded, the base is narrowly tapering, slender petiole, purple papilionaceous flowers of about 10 mm long, very fragrant that are borne on long slender stalks in terminal axillary racemes. The fruit is a samara of 4 to 5 cm long and is more or less a round nut, somewhat heavily veined, occasionally smooth, bearing a single, oblong, rather curved, and membranous wing up to 4 cm long.
Habitat and Distribution	S. longipedunculata is found in a broad range of vegetation ranging from semi-arid scrub to dense forest, including many woodland and bush habitats and gallery forests. It is widely distributed in the Sudano-Sahelian, Sudanian and Sudano-Guinean regions of Africa including Angola, Benin, Botswana, Burundi, Cameroon, Chad, Cote d'Ivoire, Democratic Republic of Congo, Eritrea, Ethiopia, Gambia, Ghana, Guinea, Kenya, Malawi, Mali, Mozambique, Namibia, Niger, Nigeria, Rwanda, Senegal, Sierra Leone, South Africa, Sudan, Tanzania, Uganda, Zambia and Zimbabwe.
Plant part of	Leaf and root bark

interest

Chemical constituents	Saponins, tannins, anthraquinones; alkaloids; terpenes; methyl salicylate; sterols, sugars, caffeic acid, sinapic acid; (Odebiyi, 1978; Kerharo and Adam, 1974; Mahmood et al., 1993; Costa et al., 1992).
Ethnomedical Uses	Decoction of the root pulp or leaves together with other plants is used to induce emesis and purgation after poisoning (Kerharo and Adam, 1974). The decoction of the crushed leaves, mixed with water is used to treat gonorrhoea, while fresh root decoction is used to treat bronchitis, stomach pain and leprosy. Root and stem bark infusions are prescribed as an antidote for poisoning. A powder made from the root is used as a snuff for headaches. In some countries like Ethiopia, smoke from burning of the root is inhaled as a medicinal incense to treat flatulence. The powdered bark is used to treat wounds and a paste of pounded bark with copper sulfate is applied to blisters caused by Guinea worm to promote expulsion and for rheumatoid arthritis, chronic rheumatism, bruises or swelling, a paste of powdered root bark is used. In West Africa, the plant is used for the treatment of infantile convulsions and combined with Boophane disticha for psychoactive purposes. The plant is known in many African countries as

	an abortifacient (Oliver-Bever, 1986).
Precaution for use	Do not exceed the recommended doses. The root has demonstrated a very low safety dose margins and self-medication is not encouraged
Dosage and Dosage form	Decoction, powders Seneginate magnesium is used in capsule 130 mg and at 2 to 10 capsules a day

40. Senna alata

Botanical Name	Senna alata
Common name	Ringworm shrub, Craw-craw plant, King of the forest, Candle stick cassia; ringworm senna; guajava; ringworm bush; seven-goldencandlesticks; Emperor's candlesticks; Empresscandle plant; christmas-candle; candlestick senna; candle bush, fleur St Christophe

Local name	Ghana: Twi – Osempe, Ga Adangbe – Bayisa, Ewe – Agbobladzoe Nigerian: Yoruba – Asunwon oyinbo, Hausa – Majamfari, Ibo – Ogalu Niger: Hausa – Sanga Sanga
	Togo: Ewe - Zangarati, Ouatchi – Zanguerati, Adja – Zangalati
Description	This is a soft-wooded shrub that is highly decorative with an interesting appearance which grows about 3 m or more in height. Its leaves are compound pinnate consisting of 8-14 pairs of oblong to obovate leaflets which are 5-16 cm long by 3-8 cm wide and are rounded at the end. The rachis are narrowly winged with a ridge connecting the leaflets. The petiole and rachis are up to 60 cm in length. The flowers are in crest terminal cymes, producing golden yellow flowers in stout, dense, erect and large, spike–like racemes with fertile stamen. Fruit which has four broad crenate wings along the middle, straight, winged along sides, contains 30-40 seeds per fruit and is measured 15–25 cm long and about 1.8 cm broad, green when unripe and black when ripe (Adjanohoun et al., 1991).
Habitat and Distribution	The plant is originally native to America but now found widely distributed throughout the tropics and in West Africa from Senegal to Nigeria (Irvine, 1961). It is a common

	plant that is found in villages, wastelands, clearings and homes; cultivated or spontaneous. In Nigeria it is found in the rain forest and the savannah, both in the southern and northern parts of the country (Elujoba and Ogunti, 1993; Adjanohoun et al., 1991).
Plant part of interest	Dried leaflets
Chemical constituents	Anthraquinones like aloe-emodin, rhein glycoside and aloe-emodin glycoside, sennosides, rhein, chrysophanic acid; tannins and mucilage (Elujoba et al, 1989; Rai and Adbullahi, 1978; Ogunti et al, 1991; GHP, 1992; Gupta, 1991).
Ethnomedical Uses	The leaves are important for treating dermatitis, eczema, ringworm, intestinal helminthiasis, taeniasis, constipation, asthma, gonorrhoea, bronchitis, delayed labour and as an abortifacient (OliverBever, 1986; Hauptman and Lacerda, 1950).
Precaution for use	High doses may influence the absorption of other drugs due to reduction in intestinal changing time. The use by nursing mothers, children under 10 years for more than 2 weeks, would require medical supervision. As with all anthranoid glycoside-containing herbs, long-term use may cause pigmentation of the intestinal

mucosa, also provoke nausea and vomiting in large doses.

| Dosage and Dosage form | Infusion: The dried pods or leaves should be placed in warm water for 6-12 hours. Then 1 teaspoon is placed in about. 150 ml of water, and is then filtered after 10 minutes. One cup is taken in the morning and/or before going to the bed. |

Powder: 1-2 g is taken with 150 ml of water (purgative)

Tincture: 1:5 is placed in 50% alcohol. 2-4 ml should be taken at bedtime.

Laxative: 3 – 4g is taken as hot infusion at bedtime.

Skin infections: 1-2% of powder is incorporated into soap or body cream.

41. Senna alexandrina

Botanical Name	Senna alexandrina
Common name	Alexandrian senna (Cassia acutifolia Del.); Tinnevelley senna (Cassia angustifolia Valil.)
Local name	Mali: Tamachek – Aghe-Agher, Egerger
	Niger: Arabic – Senna Jebeli, Senna Makha
	Nigeria: Arabic Shuwa – Senna Jebeli, Hausa – Filáskon Máká
Description	It is a small shrub with erect stack of 1 to 1.5 m high and has a compound paripinnate leaves about 10 cm in length with 3-7 pairs of leaflets which are about 12-24 cm long and 7-12 mm wide. The leaves are narrow, pale green to yellowish green in colour. The plant produce a zygomorphic flowers with yellow petals. Its fruit is elliptical, flattened and has dehiscent

	pod of 4-7 cm long and 2 cm wide, containing 6-10 seeds per pod (WHO, 1999; African Pharmacopoeia, 1985; Wallis, 1967).
Habitat and Distribution	It is found in upper Nile territories, Alexandria, Sudan and other semi-desert zones of Africa.
Plant part of interest	Leaf
Chemical constituents	Contains hydroxyanthracene glycosides particularly Sennosides A, B, C and D, aloe-emodin, rhein – 8-glucosides, mucilage and flavonoids (African pharmacopoeia, 1985; Wallis, 1967), Sennocides A, B, C (Okafor et al., 2001).
Ethnomedical Uses	It is used for bowel evacuation, constipation, liver disease, jaundice, anaemia, splenomegally and typhoid
Precaution for use	High doses may influence the absorption of other drugs due to reduction in intestinal transit time. Except on medical advice, it should not be used for more than 14 days or for children under the age of 10 years (British Pharmacopoiea, 1988; Godding, 1998).
Dosage and Dosage form	When used as laxative, 0.5-2.0 g should be taken at bed time as hot tea, and as purgative: 2-4 g should be taken at bed time as hot tea

42. Senna occidentalis

Botanical Name	Senna occidentalis
Common name	Coffee senna, Mogdad coffee, stinkweed (English); Herbe puante, Casse fétide (French); Fedegosa (Portuguese)
Local name	Buirkina Faso: Mooré – Kinkéliba, Dioula – M'balan m'balan;mbala fin, Fulfuldé – Tasbati
	Cote d'Ivoire: Baoulé – Aloukou Sere Sere, Malinké – Badjaa; Akyé – M'bechilè
	Gambia: Mandinka – Kassala, Fulla – Tiga Sowru, Wollof – Hobi Ghana: Akan – Mmofraborodee, Ga Dangme – Gbekebii Arnadaa, Ewe – Dzongbale
	Mali: Bambara – N'Balan Balanfing,

Noms – Tasbati, Malinké – Kassé

Niger: Djerma – Sanga Sanga, Hausa – Raydoré

Nigeria: Yoruba – Rere

Senegal: Serer – Ben Fènè; Bénékèné, Wolof – Bantamaré, Diola – Bufata

Sierra Leone: Kisi – Dilankido, Shebro – Sabibosueleh, Temne – E-Bambaforke

Togo: Ewé – Bessissan, Ouatchi – Avakofè; Adja – Laloui

Description	It is an annual herb or undershrub that may survive for up to three years. Its leaves are compound pinnate, leaflets are 4-5 pairs, terminal pair largest, broadly lanceolate or ovate and can be 3.5-10 cm long, 3-4 cm broad, apex acute, gland near base of leaf rachis. Flowers are yellow, fruit is linear pod, somewhat flattened and abruptly beaked.
Habitat and Distribution	Common weed found on wasteland in villages and towns and on roadsides and it is pantropical
Plant part of interest	Leaf
Chemical constituents	Anthraquinone (e.g. the sennosides, chrysophanol, physcion, helminthosporin, emodin), fatty oils,

	flavonoids ((jaceine 7rhamnoside, mattencinol 7-rhamnoside, matteucinol 7-rhamnoside, jaceidin-7rhamnoside, cassiaoccidentalins A, B and C), xanthones (cassiollin); gallactomannan, polysaccharides and tannins) (Chukwujekwu et al., 2006; Purwar et al., 2003; Hatano et al., 1999; Ikram et al., 1978; Glasby, 1991; Gupta et al., 2005).
Ethnomedical Uses	S. occidentalis is used in many places in Africa to treat a range of conditions which incude abscesses, bruises, cataracts, constipation, eye infections, headache, jaundice, kidney infections, leprosy, malaria, kidney pain, menstrual disorders, rheumatism, ringworm, scabies, sore throat, stomach ulcers, stomachache, syphilis, tetanus, worms, fevers, tuberculosis, anaemia, liver, disorders; general weakness, asthma; bronchitis and venereal diseases (Chukwujekwu et al., 2005; Tona et al., 2004; Samy and Ignacimuthu, 2000;). In Mali, the leaves are used for treatment of oedema and a decoction is prepared for malaria, fevers in pregnancy, yellow fever, headache and conjunctivitis. The seeds are brewed to make coffee-like beverage for asthma, hypertension, malaria, fevers and stomach complaints
Precaution for	The fluid extract from the plant can cause hypoglycaemia and increased

use	liver and kidney function. Hepatic and renal blood glucose level need to be regularly monitored on prolonged use
Dosage and Dosage form	Decoction: 10 g of dried powdered leaves should be placed in 500 ml water. One teacup should be taken two times daily. Tincture: 1:5 should be placed in 50% ethanol. Five ml should be taken three times daily

43. Senna podocarpa

Botanical Name	Senna podocarpa
Common name	Podocarpa leaf
Local name	Cote d'Ivoire: Baule – Niaaka Niabaka, Kru Guere – Siogelebe, Sioguele Belebel Kweni Gambia: Manding Mandinka – Kanayiro Ghana: Akan – Sreso Simpe, Ga –

Nyonbele, Wasa – Nsuduru Guinea: Basari – Mbokwe, Fula Pulaar – Yeleuk, Konyagi – Mpman Guinea Bissau: Manding Mandink – Adjam, Djam-Cafae, Pepel - Beuroque

Liberia: Mano - Ba La Bli

Nigeria: Igbo – Gaalu, Igbo (Agulu) – Ogaala, Yoruba – asunwon anago, peiebe.

Senegal: Balanta – Banban, Diola – Bunan Bunangabo, Fula - Bendiagkafara

Sierra-Leone: Kono – Wawa, Loko – Balaga, Temne – E-Ai-Ani

Description   A glabrous shrub that can grow up to 5 m high. Its leaves are pinnately compound and sometimes imparipinnate. Petiole and rachis are up to 30 cm long. There are 4-5 pairs of leaflets which are elliptic with narrowed ends and are 6-12 cm long, 3-6 cm broad. The flowers appear between October and December and are light yellow in colour. Inflorescence has a dense, erect, spike-like terminal raceme. The fruits are pods, not winged, straight, flat, centrally attached and become brownish-black when ripe, normally shiny, flatbeaked and slightly curved with transverse ridges. The fruit can grow up to 10-12 cm long and about

	1.5 cm wid and forms indehiscent fruit pods. The plant produces fruit between November and January. Seeds are as numerous as 14-16 per pod and are dark-brown to black in colour, smooth, hard and oblong, with a pointed edge (Irvine, 1961).
Habitat and Distribution	The plant is found in Guinea savannah and in secondary clearings, in wastelands and sometimes cultivated in homes. The plant is distributed from Senegal to Nigeria but however restricted to the rain forest zones of Nigeria namely: Benin, IleIfe, Olokemeji, Ibadan, Lagos and Nsukka. Not generally found in the Northern and Upper Eastern parts of Nigeria (Dalziel, 1936).
Plant part of interest	Fresh and dried leaflets
Chemical constituents	The plant is rich in anthracene glycosides, O-and-C-anthraquinone glycosides and free anthraquinones (emodin).
Ethnomedical Uses	The plant is applied in folklore as a purgative, labour stimulant, anti-gonorrhoeal, guinea worm expellant, emmenagogue and ecbolic (Anton and Haag-Berriere, 1980).
Precaution for use	Excessive use may cause diarrhoea, abdominal colic, dehydration, bogy

	weakness, loss of weight and damage to the myenteric plexus. Use for more than 2 weeks or on children under the age of 10 years requires medical supervision.
Dosage and Dosage form	Decoction: 30 g of the dried leaflets is placed in 900 ml water. This is allowed to simmer until it is reduced to 600 ml. Then 1-3 cups should be taken daily
	Infusion: 30 g of the dried leaves is placed in 600 ml of water. Then 13 cups should be taken daily.
	Tincture- 1:5 is placed in 50% alcohol, and 5 ml to be taken three times daily.

44. Solanum torvum

Botanical Name	Solanum torvum

Common name	Solanum (English), Fausse aubergine; aubergine sauvage (French
Local name	Ghana: Akan- Kwao Nsuswaa Cote d'Ivoire: Kyama- Guiguisuron Nigeria: Edo- Omgbabelara, Yoruba- asimonwu Sierra Leone: Kono- Kōlau
Description	This is an erect shrub, that grows up to 3.55 m tall. Its stem is pale green in colour and is armed with flat scattered spines. The leaves are alternate, ovate to oblong-ovate, pinnately lobed in shape and 7-19 cm long, 518 cm broad. There are isstellate hairs on both surfaces of the leaves and the petiole is 1-4 cm long, and is also armed with 1-3 cm spines. Inflorescence is laterally arranged usually with extra axillary racemose and often dichotomous. The flowers on the inflorescence are many, white or lilac coloured and is about 1 cm long. Corolla tube is short with 5-lobed limb. Stamens are four, filaments short, anthers united into a cone, ovary is 2-celled; fruit is round is 1-15 mm diameter and is green in colour but turns pale orange when ripe.
Habitat and Distribution	The plant originates from Central and South America, where it occurs in Mexico, Brazil and Peru, and is also widespread in the Caribbean. It is now

a tropical weed; in West and Central Africa it used as kitchen garden crop, and may occurs in other regions of Africa. S. torvum grows on open land in distorted soil, on roadsides, brushy pastures, recently farmland, river banks and wastelands, where it often becomes a weed that becomes difficult to control. In Cameroon it is a pioneer species on fallow land. It is listed as a noxious weed in the south-eastern United States. It is normally found either near wetlands or in high rainfall areas, mainly in lowland regions, but is tolerant of dry periods. It grows well in full sunlight,

Plant part of interest	Fruit

Chemical constituents

The plant is rich in isoflavonoid (torvanol A), steroidal glycoside (torvoside H); neochlorogenin 6-O-β-Dquinovopyranoside, neochlorogenin-6-O-β-Dxylopyranosyl-(1→3)-β-D-quinovopyranoside, neochlorogenin-6-O-α-L-rhamnopyranosyl(1→3)-β-D-quinovopyranoside, solagenin-6-O-β

D D-quinovopyranoside, solagenin-6-O-α-Lrhamnopyranosyl-(1→3)-β-D-quinovopyranoside, isoquercetin, rutin, kaempferol; quercetin; alkaloids (solasodine, soagenin), tannins (Kusirisin et al., 2009; Yuan-Yuan et al., 2011; Pérez-Amador et al., 2007;

	Arthan et al., 2006).
Ethnomedical Uses	Fruits, flowers and stems possess carminative, anthelmintic and bitter properties. The root is expectorant and used to treat chest pain due to cough, asthma and bronchitis. The leaves are applied externally as a pain reliever. Different parts of the plant are used worldwide as an antidote for poison and for the treatment of fever, wounds, tooth ache, gastric ulceration, skin diseases, reproductive disorders, fever and arterial hypertension (Noumi et al., 1999; Muthu et al., 2006; Kala, 2005). In the treatment of female infertility, 3 or 4 g of the fruit are macerated in palm wine and administered orally (Telefo et al., 2011). The fruits are boiled with leaves and a cupful of the decoction drunk to treat malaria (Asase et al., 2010). The leaves are used in Central America, India, and Gabon to treat cuts and wounds and diabetes. In Sierra Leone, the fruit decoction is given to children suffering from cough, whereas in Senegal the plant is used to treat sore throat and stomachache. The decoction is drunk to treat indigestion, gastric pain at the navel, rheumatism, numbness, contusion, lumbar muscular pains, and amenorrhoea. Decoction is used in some areas to lessen postpartum haemorrhage.
Precaution for	The unripe fruits are reported to be

use	poisonous.
Dosage and Dosage form	Decoction of 15 to 30 gm dried roots, or processed into syrup or alcoholic suspension

45. Sorghum bicolor

Botanical Name	Sorghum bicolor
Common name	Great millet, Guinea corn, sweet sorghum (English), Sorgho (French).
Local name	Burkina Faso: Mooré – Baninga ou kazieega, Dioula – Gnô wilé, Fulfuldé – Bayéri;ghaouri
	Ghana: Dagare – Kazu Kpulekpule, Dagbani – Chi, Akan – Atoko Mali: Bambara – Kenegue, Dogon – Eme, Senoufos – Kale Gue Nigeria: Hausa – Chi Nduka, Kanuri – Mbio, Yoruba – Oka baba Togo: Ewe – Adako, Mina – Ada, Ouatchi – Adadzen
Description	This is a cane-like grass that grows up

to 6 m tall and forms large branched clusters of grains but the individual grains are small, about 3-4 mm in diameter. They vary in colour from pale yellow through reddish brown to dark brown depending on the kind. Most of the kinds are annuals, only few are perennials. It is a cultivated plant and mostly nonrhizomatous. The culms nodes are either glabrous or shortly tomentose. It has inflorescence is contracted and has alternate branches.

Habitat and Distribution	Sorghum bicolor is an African crop, and is widely distributed worldwide. Different kinds are found in different regions depending on the climatic condition of the area. However, it is adapted to a wider range of ecological conditions and is mostly a plant of hot, dry regions. It still strive in cool weather as well as waterlogged habitats
Plant part of interest	Leaf
Chemical constituents	Alkaloids (hordenine), saponins, phytates, phenols, tannins, hydrocyanic acid, quinone, sorgoleone, dihydrosorgoleone, fibre; proteins, carbohydrates, saturated and unsaturated fatty acids (Mehmood et al., 2008; Oladiji et al., 2007; Barbosa et al., 2001).

Ethnomedical Uses	It is found to be antiabortive, cyanogenetic, diuretic, emollient, intoxicant, and poison, and a folk remedy for cancer, epilepsy and stomachache (Duke and Wain, 1981). The root is used for malaria in Zimbabwe and the seed is indicated for breast disorders and diarrheoa and the stem for tubercular swellings. In countries like India, the plant is considered as an anthelminthic and insecticidal. In South Africa, the plant in combination with Erigeron canadense L., is used for eczema. In China, the seeds are used to make alcohol and the seed husk is braised in brown sugar with a little water and applied to the chest of measles patients. The seeds are found to be beneficial in fluxes (Perry, 1980). The leaf decoction is used to treat measles (Morton (1981), while a powdered mixture of the seeds and the calabash tree used in the treatment of lung ailments. In Venezuela, the seeds are toasted and pulverized for diarrhoea while in Brazil the seed decoction is used for bronchitis, cough and other chest ailments. Hot oil packs of the seeds are applied to the back of patients with pulmonary congestion. Grieve (1984), recommends that a decoction of about 50 g seed be boiled in a liter of water to about 1/2 liter for the treatment of kidney and urinary

	disorders.
Precaution for use	Caution should be taken in infant patients
Dosage and Dosage form	Infusion: about 25 g is taken per day
	Fluid extract: about 25 ml is taken daily.
	Tincture: 1:5, 90% alcohol 0.3-1.2 ml, max 25 ml taken per week

46. Spathodea campanulata

Botanical Name	Spathodea campanulata
Common name	English: African tulip tree, Flame tree, Fountain tree, Uganda flame, Nile flame, Nandi flame French: Tulipier d'Africain, Arbre flamme, Bâton de sorcier
Local name	Burkina Faso: Fulfuldé –

Djapelede;kafavano

Ghana: Akan – Akuakuoninsuo

Nigeria: Bokyi – Kenshie

Senegal: Balanta – Blalo

Togo: Ewe – Adatsigo, Fon – Dudu, Ouatchi – Adassigolo

Description	This is a dioecious tree that reaches about 35 m tall. It often occurs in the form of bush savanna, shallow-rooted, fluted, measuring about 60 cm in diameter. Its bark is grey, pale brown and smooth, becoming dark grey with age and it is rough and scaly at the base of the barrel. The leaves are opposite or in whorls of 3 three, odd-pinnate, without stipules. Inflorescence is in terminal raceme and the flowers is bisexual. The fruit is narrowly ellipsoid, measuring from 15 to 27 cm long and is dehiscent by 2 valves
Habitat and Distribution	It is found growing in many African countries such as Ghana, Nigeria, Cameroon, Guinea, Angola, Congo, Sudan, Uganda and Senegal. It also occurs in deciduous forests, woodlands and savanna forest edges and commonly grown as a street tree.
Plant part of interest	Stem bark

Chemical constituents	Ferulic acid, vanillic acid, verminoside (6-Ocaffeoyl-catalpol: iridoid glycoside), stachyose(O-α-D-galactopyranosyl-(1-6)-O-α-Dgalactopyranosyl-(1-6)-O-α-D-glucopyranosyl-(12)-β-D-fructofuranoside; spathoside, (new cerebroside), spathodea acid, triterpenes: 3β,19α,24-trihydroxyolean-12-ene-28-oic acid), oleanolic acid, 3β-acetoxy-oleanolic acid, βsitosterol-3-O-β-d-glucopyranoside; quercetin, caffeic acid; siaresinolique acid, 3β-acetoxyoleanolic acid, β-sitosterol-3-O-β-dglucopyranoside, β-sitosterol, spathodol (sterol hydroxylated); cyanidin-3-O-rutinoside, pelargonidin-3-O-rutinoside; pomolic acid, phydroxybenzoic acid esters and phenylethanol; octacosanol and triacontanol (Gorman et al., 2004; Niyonzima, 1997; Mbosso et al., 2008; Silvere et al., 1990).
Ethnomedical Uses	Many parts of the plant body are used in African traditional medicine for the treatment of a diseases, including dysentery, gastritis, ulcers, pelvic pain in women, headache, oedema, dermatitis, guinea worm. The stem bark is applied to treat wounds (Mensah et al., 2003). The macerated leaf is used to treat urethritis and as an antidote for poison. The bark decoction is used for kidney disorders, swelling and skin complaints (Irvin,

	1961). The stem bark is used as an enema in diabetes (Niyonzima, 1997). The macerated bark of the trunk is a cure for infectious diseases including sexually transmitted diseases (Magassouba et al., 2007). In Ghana, the plant is used for the treatment of dyspepsia, peptic ulcer, fracture, toothache, stomach ache and stomach ulcer (Agbovie et al., 2002).
Precaution for use	No precautions that is specifically required within the recommended dose of the aqueous extract.
Dosage and Dosage form	Infusion: about 25 g is taken per day Tincture: 1:5, 90% alcohol 0.3-1.2 ml, max 25 ml per week

47. Spermacoce verticillata

Botanical Name	Spermacoce verticillata

Common name	Buttonweeds, African borreria (English); Borreria verte, Borrerie verticillée (French)
Local name	Burkina Faso: Fulfuldé – Gurdudal
	Mali: Bambara – Missini Koumbere, Peuhl – Samtarde
	Nigeria: Yoruba – Irawo-Ile
	Senegal: Wolof – Ndatukan, Bu Gôr; Serer – Murah, Faduala, Diola – Karibun, Eribun
Description	Plant like sub-shrub, perennial, 1 m high and is branched. It has a hairless stems with stipular sheaths that are smooth or rough. Leaves are glabrous, oblanceolate up to 4 cm by 7 mm with lateral veins, not very prominent. Infloressence is spherical, compact, terminal and axillary and can be 10 to 15 mm in diameter, usually with two leafy bracts about 1 cm long which curved downwards. It has a small white flowers. Fruit is a drupe, dry, dehiscent.
Habitat and Distribution	The plant is distributed extensively across the Sudano-Guinean region and part of the Sahel especially along the West African coast and along the coast of South America and Madagascar.
Plant part of interest	Leaf, root, aerial parts

Chemical constituents	Contains essential oil (sesquiterpene hydrocarbons, sesquiterpene lactones, phenolic compounds and aromatic polycarboxylic acids), azulene alkaloids (borrérine and borrévérine) iridoids and iridosides (daphylloside 1, 2 asperuloside, feretoside 3, 4 methyl desacetylasperulosidate, aspéruloside, férétoside, daphyloside and asperulosidic acid acid 7) [African Pharmcopoeia, 1985].
Ethnomedical Uses	The plant is traditionally used to treat leprosy, boils, syphilis, gonorrhoea and schistosomiasis. The root is used as a diuretic and laxative. Leaves and roots are used to treat vaginal discharge, impotence, and haemorrhoids (Paulino de Albuquerque et al., 2007). The plant is used to treat inflammation (Gazzaneo et al., 2005) and as an insecticide (Rohrig et al., 2008). The decoction of the bark is administered orally to treat infectious diseases including sexually transmitted infections (Magassouba et al., 2007).
Precaution for use	The plant must be administered orally with caution.
Dosage and Dosage form	Internally: it is used as tea, essential oil, capsules. Externally: usually used as topical skin application such as lotions, tinctures,

ointments, pastes.

Decoction: 30 g of the plant material is placed in 900 ml water, simmer until it reduced to 600 ml. 1 tablespoonful is administered two times daily.

48. Spondias mombin

Botanical Name	Spondias mombin
Common name	English: Hog plum (English), Mombin, Prune mombin ou Prune Myrobolan (French)
Local name	Burkina Faso: Dioula – Mingo; Minkon, Fulfuldé – Talé;tali
	Cote d'Ivoire: Abe – Ngba
	Ghana: Twi – Atoaa Mali: Barbara – Minko Mingo Ninkom, Peul – Talé tali, Dogon – Enye Vevey
	Nigeria: Yoruba – Agliko Senegal:

	Wolof – Sob ninkôm, Serer – Yoga, Diola – Bu lila Bu lilu
	Togo: Ewe – Akoukonti, Adja – Kukon, Adele – Inyanya
Description	It grows 15 - 25 m high with a clear bark, cracked, rough and thick. The bark is usually covered with large spines and releases resin upon injury. The drum thickened at the base, reaching about 0.75 m in diameter. The branches are flared and the foliage is full and balanced. Leaves are compound, odd-pinnate, measuring 50 cm long with 5-8 pairs of leaflets 7 cm long and 3.5 cm wide, short rib at the edge of the lamina uniting the lateral veins. It has small white flowers, fragrant with large terminal panicles appearing during the dry season defoliation. Inflorescences are arranged in terminal panicles and are 20 to 40 cm long, covered with short hairs majorly. Fruit is a sweet astringent plum, pulpit more or less acidic and pleasant, have ovoid drupes from 2.5 to 4 cm long and 2 to 2.5 cm wide.
Habitat and Distribution	Found in tropical Americas, including the West Indies, but it is naturalized in parts of Africa, India and Indonesia. It is hardly cultivated. It grows well in warm weather and on a wide variety of soils.

Plant part of interest	Stem bark and leaf
Chemical constituents	Tannins, palmitic, linoleic, oleic, stearic, linolenic acids, flavonoids (quercetin, quercetrin, rutin, and their 7-O-glucosides), saponin, sugars; alkaloids, proanthocyanins (condensed tannins) (Moronkola et al., 2003; Apori et al., 1998)
Ethnomedical Uses	In Mali, the plant is used to treat teeth decay. It is also used as a diuretic, laxative and purgative and febrifuge (Adjanohoun et al., 1979). The leaf extracts have potent antimicrobial and antifungal properties. The juice obtained by expression of the fresh leaves is commonly used in the treatment of eye diseases, while the leaf or root bud decoction is prescribed for diarrhoea and dysentery or macerated for colic pain (Kerharo and Adam, 1974). The decoction of the leaves with salt is known to has diuretic and laxative properties (Adjanohoun et al, 1979). The leaf decoction is also a remedy for caries, dental problems, colic, various eye diseases and toothache (Boullard, 2001). The bark infusion is used in mouthwash to prevent toothache and as an anthelmintic. The decoction of the bark is used in cough with severe inflammatory symptoms, and vomiting. The dried bark is used to be sprayed on fresh wounds of

	circumcision and the stem bark is used as a tea for pregnant women (Boullard, 2001).
Precaution for use	It should not be used at greater doses. Regularly monitor blood glucose, hepatic and renal biochemical parameters on prolonged use at low doses. Should not be combined with other hypoglycaemic drugs except under medical supervision.
Dosage and Dosage form	Infusion: about 25 g is taken per day Tincture: 1:5, 90% alcohol 0.3-1.2 ml, max 25 ml per week

49. Tetrapleura tetraptera

Botanical Name	Tetrapleura tetraptera
Common name	Tetrapleura pod, Tétrapleura à 4 ailes (French).

Local name	Ghana: Akan – Prekese
	Nigeria: Yuroba – Aridan, Hausa – Kalangun daji, Igbo – Shosho
Description	This is a perennial, deciduous forest tree of about 20 m tall and 3 m girth, with fern-like foliage and dark green leaves which usually lack buttresses. It possesses slender crown, leaves are composite, bipinnate and are about 5-10 pairs of alternate leaflets. Leaves are oblong-elliptic, sub-sessile, pubescent at lower side and have smooth bark. greyish, very thin, slash reddish and strong smelling. It is practically glabrous or have minutely hairy twigs and young foliage with common stalk 15–30 cm long which is slightly channelled on the upper surface and the leaflets are 6–12 in number on each side of pinna-stalk are always alternate. The veins are lateral and indistinct, running at a wide angle to the prominent midrib. Inflorescence is in axiliary spike. The flowers are creamy or pink, turning orange, densely crowded in spike-like racemes 5–20 cm long. Individual flowers have slender stalks and have about 20 short stamens. Fruits are persistent, hanging at the end of branches on stout stalks and are 15–25 cm long and about 5 cm across the winged ribs of the pods which are dark, reddish-brown or dark purple-brown to black in colour when ripe

	but greenish when unripe, glabrous and glossy, usually curved and about 15 cm long. Two of the wings are hard and woody and the other two filled with a soft pulp; seeds are hard, black, flat oval, about 0.75 cm long, embedded in the body of the pod, which does not split, black-shelled but bright-green inside containing oil (Burkill, 1995; Adjanahoun et al., 1991).
Habitat and Distribution	The plant is commonly fpund on the fringe of the West African rainforest belt, particularly secondary forest. The species is found throughout the upper forest zone, southern savanna-woodland especially in Benin, Burkina Faso, Cambodia, Cameroon, Chad, Ghana, Guinea, Liberia, Mali, Mauritania, Niger, Nigeria, Senegal, Sierra Leone, Togo and Uganda (Burkill, 1995).
Plant part of interest	Fruit
Chemical constituents	Aminopropionic acid derivatives, terpenoids (aridanin), alkaloids (mimosine), flavonoids, cinnamic acids, caffeic acid, tannins, terpenes, fixed oils, carbohydrates, and triglycoside (Adewunmi, 1999; Adesina and Reisch, 1985)
Ethnomedical	The plant is useful in the treatment of convulsion, leprosy oedema,

Uses	rheumatic pains, female sterility and inflammation. The bark decoction is used for treating cough, bronchitis, menstrual pains and arthritis and the root decoction is used for jaundice. Aqueous extract of the pod is used as anticonvulsant whilst its paste is used to treat rheumatism. The intense odour on roasting is claimed to possess insect- and snake-repellent properties (Gill, 1992). In some parts of West Africa, the fruit is used as a a spice or as a source of multivitamins. In eastern parts of Nigeria, fruits serves as soups for mothers from the first day of delivery to prevent postpartum contraction.
Precaution for use	No special precautions required within the recommended dose of the aqueous extract
Dosage and Dosage form	Infusion: about 25 g is taken per day Decoction: 300 g of crushed fruit is boiled with 900 ml of water until is reduced to 600 ml. Then, take two tablespoonfuls twice daily Tincture: 1:5, 90% alcohol 0.3-1.2 ml, max 25 ml per week

50. Tinospora bakis

Botanical Name	Tinospora bakis
Common name	Tinospora (English), Bakis (French)
Local name	Burkina Faso: Mooré – Bésindé, Fulfuldé – Bakañi;bakañé
	Ghana: Kusasi – Ba Ila Nigeria: Igbo – Aga Oyi
	Senegal: Wolof–Bakis, Sérère-Péis,Peuhl–Abolo
Description	The plant is twining herbaceous or shrubby perennial that reaches 10-15 m high. Its stems are vines, climbers, glabrous, topped with very large white lenticels. The roots are tuberous, has sap which is translucent. The leaves are simple and alternate and broadly ovate. The base is strung, summit shortly acuminate and the petiole is 2 to 8 cm long. The flowers are greenish-yellow which are arranged in

	axillary racemes, measuring 3 to 10 cm long. The male flowers are small, with 9 cm long and 4 to 5 mm wide, rounded with three sepals borne on pedicels that is 3 to 5 mm. Fruits are small berries greenish in colour, oval, 1 cm long, bulge at the base, apiculate at the summit, pedicels 8 to 10 mm.
Habitat and Distribution	The plant is distributed on the banks of rivers in some regions of sub-Saharan Africa, and is mostly encountered in Senegal, Mali, Mauritania, Niger, Northern Nigeria, in eastern Sudan, Ethiopia and Angola
Plant part of interest	Root/rhizome
Chemical constituents	Alkaloids (columbine), (Oyen, 2008); steroidal glycosides; saponins, tannins, coumarins, anthocyanins, carotenoids, fatty acids, polysaccharides and reducing sugars.
Ethnomedical Uses	The plant is taken orally for the treatment of jaundice, fever, severe malaria, menstrual disorders, schistosomiasis, dermatitis, and poor vision (Oyen, 2008; Kerharo and Adam, 1974).
Precaution for use	Do not exceed prescribed doses as high doses caused toxic effects
Dosage and Dosage form	Decoction, Bitters 200 gm of powdered plant material boiled with 1000 ml of water until reduced to 600

ml. Take two tablespoonfuls twice daily.

51. Vernonia colorata

Botanical Name	Vernonia colorata
Common name	Bitter leaf (English), Quinine des noirs (French).
Local name	Burkina Faso: Mooré – koa-safandé, Dioula – Khô safouné, Fulfuldé – Ndumburkhat, Mossi – Kosa Safandé, Bambara – Ko Safna
	Cote d'Ivoire: Agni – Baoulé Abovi Abowi Aovi, Akyé – Todzo, Malinké – Kosafna
	Mali: Bambara – Ko-Safina, Malinké – Ko-Safina
	Nigeria: Hausa – Shiwaka, Yoruba – Ewuro, Edo – Owiro

	Senegal: Wolof – Ndumburghat Zidor, Diola – Ka Sipa, Serer – Mam Mbumkarkap
	Togo: Ewé – Aloma, Ouatchi – Alo, Adja – Alotsi
Description	Vernonia colorata is a highly branched shrub or tree that can grow up to 3-5 m high. The leaves are pubescent, ovate-elliptic, 8-15 cm long and 5-10 cm broad and have undulate margins. The upper surface of thr leaves is harshly hairy and the undersurface is covered in dense woolly hairs. Petiole is 15-30 mm long, pubescent. Inflorescences is flattened panicles and composed of small capitulum of 5 to 15 cm long. Flower is white or bluish, tubular 8-10 mm, achenes glabrous, with reddish brown pappus, 3 mm long (Ake Assi and Guinko, 1986).
Habitat and Distribution	The plant grows in savana and rain forests, especially in secondary growth and wet places. It is found in most West African, Central African and South African tropical countries.
Plant part of interest	Leaf
Chemical constituents	Amino acids, Vitamin C, carotenoid, iron, sesquiterpene lactones (vernolide, hydroxyvernolide,19-hydroxyglaucolide A, vernodalin derivatives) (Ejoh et al., 2005a, Ejoh

	et al., 2005b; Senatore et al., 2004).
Ethnomedical Uses	The plant is one of the widely consumed edible leaf vegetables found in West Africa and Cameroon. The leaves have a sweet and bitter taste. The plant has long been used in traditional medicine for the treatment of cough, fever, hepatitis, stomachache, diabetes, colic, rheumatism, dysentery, ulcerative colitis, venereal diseases, diarrhoea, boils and skin eruptions (Hutchings et al., 1996). Leaf infusions or decoctions are used as mouth wash for tonsillitis, earache and fever. The fresh leaf extract is applied to wounds (Kerharo and Adam, 1974; Ake Assi and Guinko, 1986; Oliver-Bever, 1996; Adjanohoun et al., 1985).
Precaution for use	Excessive ingestion may cause diarrhoea
Dosage and Dosage form	Decoction: boil 40 g of dried leaves per litre for 15 minutes. Drink 4 teacapfuls three time a day

52. Zingiber officinale

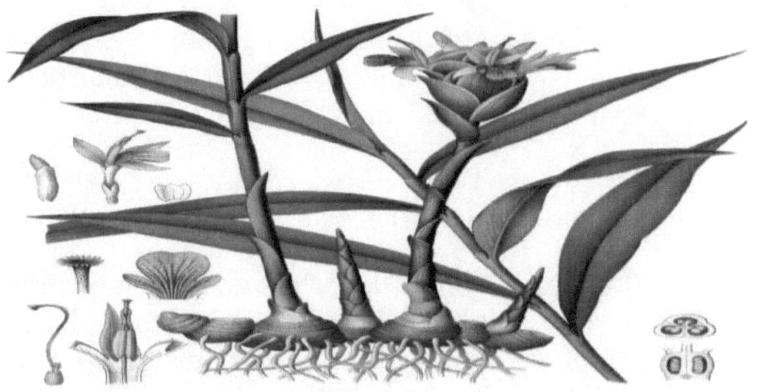

Botanical Name	Zingiber officinale
Common name	Ginger (English), Gingembre (French).
Local name	Burkina Faso: Mooré – Gnamaku, Dioula – Dougouma niamako, Fulfuldé – Gnamakou Bobo – Dugumo nyamugu
	Ghana: Adangbe – Odzahwi, Akan – Akakador Tsintsimir, Dagbani - Sakarra Tschibilli
	Guinea: Fula Pulaar – Niamaku, Limba - A-Mbir, Manding Maninka - Niamaku Susu
	Guinea-Bissau: Crioulo - Gengipe Liberia: Mano - Ge Su
	Nigeria: Arabic Shuwa – Sakanjabir, Birom – Syataa, Yoruba – Atale. Senegal: Bedik – Nyamaku, Manding Bambara – Dugukoro Ni Amaku,

Wolof – Dinjar.

Sierra Leone: Bulom – Wischa, Bulom – Lone, Yalunka – Nyakhamuna

Togo: Anyi Anufo – Kaka'dolo, Bassari – Afu, Kabere – Wessuguae.

Description

Ginger has rhizome and is perennial plant which is of two kinds. There is one with an erect stems of 1-1.5 m in height with linear lanceolate, alternate, smooth, sheathing leaves, which die off each year, greenish pale colour(stem is sterile). The other is about 20 cm or less in height (stems is sterile, carrying sheath of bracts) with short, yellowish-green flowers, ending in a long curve spike. Each of the flower shows a superior tubular calyx, orange-yellow corolla with three lobes and inferior 3-celled ovary with tufted stigma. Fruit is a capsule with small argillite seeds. Rhizome is branched, spreads and proliferates underground (WHO, 1999; Gill, 1992).

Habitat and Distribution

This is the plant that is found in the tropics, and is especially abundant in Indo-Malaysia. The main world producers include Fiji, India, Jamaica, Nigeria, Sierra Leone and China, is cultivated in commercially quantity in nearly every tropical and sub-tropical country of the world.

Plant part of interest	Rhizome
Chemical constituents	Contains volatile oil (oleo-resin), monoterpenes (8-phellandrene, camphene, cineole, citral and borneol); sesquiterpenes (zingiberene, bisabolene), gingerols, vitamin B group (niacin, ribloflavin, thiamin), vitamin C; reducing sugars, phosphatidic acids, lecithins, folic acid, mucilage (GHP, 1992; Seukawa et al, 1984).
Ethnomedical Uses	Ginger is used to treat wide range of diseases including rectal prolapse, toothache, voice hoarseness, cough, colds, flu, pregnancy-induced nausea and vomiting, asthma, fever, colic, dysmenorrhoea, diarrhoea, arthritis, hepatitis, dyspepsia (Samy, 2005; Milt and Bone, 2001; Adjanahoun et al, 1985; BHP, 1983).
Precaution for use	Excess doses should not be avoided in order to reduce the risk of cardiac arrhythmias and CNS depression. It should be used with caution in patient with gallstones and haemorrhagic conditions. It may be used in pregnancy under medical supervision
Dosage and Dosage form	For most purposes a typical dose of ginger is 1-4 g daily, taken in divided doses. Infusion: fresh root is infused for 5

minutes. Then 1 teaspoonis taken is used daily.

Decoction: put 1-1.5 teaspoonfuls of the powder in a cup of water. Tincture: 1:2 in 75% alcohols, 0.25-5 ml is taken three times a day. Capsules: 1 or 2 x 200 mg Oil. Take 1-2 drops on a sugar lump or in a teaspoon of honey.

REFERENCE

Abbiw D. K. (1990). Useful plants of Ghana, Royal botanique garden, Kew edition, 126-247.

Abel, C., Busia, K. (2005). An exploratory ethnobotanical study of the practice of Herbal Medicine by the Akan People of Ghana. Alternative Medicine Review, p 42.

Adebayo, J.O., Krettli, A.U. (2011). Potential antimalarials from Nigerian plants: A review. Journal of Ethnopharmacology 133:289–302

Abubakar, M.S., Musa, A.M., Ahmede, A., Hussaini, I.M. (2007). The perception and practice of traditional medicine in the treatment of cancers and inflammations by the Hausa and Fulani tribes of Northern Nigeria Journal of Ethnopharmacology 111:625–629

Adegbola, O.R. (1986). Establishment of Pharmacopoeial Standards for Khaya senegalensis A. Juss. and Piper guineense Schum. and Thonn. M.Phil. (Pharmacognosy) Thesis University of Ife (now Obafemi Awolowo University), Ile-Ife Nigeria.

Adeneye, A.A., Agbaje, E.O. (2007). Hypoglycemic and hypolipidemic effects of fresh leaf aqueous extract of Cymbopogon citratus Stapf. in rats. Journal of Ethnopharmacology 112:440-444.

Adesogan, E.K., Adesida, G.A., Taylor, D.A.H. (1967). Extractives from Khaya senegalensis. Chemical Communications 16:790-791.

Addy, M. (2003). Cryptolepis: An African Traditional Medicine that Provides Hope for Malaria Victims. HerbalGram 60:54-59, 67.

Adebayo, J.O., Yakubu, M.T., Egwim, E.C., Owoyele, V.B., Enaibe, B.U. (2003). Effect of ethanolic extract of Khaya senegalensis on some biochemical parameters of rat kidney.

Journal of   Ethnopharmacology 88(1):69-72

Adesina, S.K., Reisch, J. (1985). A triterpenoid glycoside from Tetrapleura tetraptera fruit.   Phytochemistry 24:3003-3006

Adewunmi C. O. (1999). Medicinal Plants, Parasites and Snails in Health. Inaugural Lecture, Series   132, Obafemi Awolowo University, Ile-Ife, Nigeria

Adjanohoun, E, et al., (1991). Contribution to ethnobotanical and floristic studies in western Nigeria. published   by   the Scientific, Technical and Research Commission of the Organisation of African Unity (OAU/STRC), Lagos

Adjanohoun, E., Ahyi, M.R.A., Ake Assi, L. et al. (1974). Contribution aux études ethnobotaniques et   floristiques en République populaire du Congo. Agence de coopération culturelle et   technique, (A.C.C.T.), Paris, 605 p., (1988) A partir de la banque de données Pharmel 2 (réf.   HP 10).

Adjanohoun, F.J., Ake, A., Floret, J.J., Guinko, S. et al., (1985). Contribution aux etudes ethnohotaniques   et floristiques du Mali Médecine Traditionnelle et Pharmacopée. ACCT, Paris

Adjanohoun, E. et al., (1991). Contribution to Ethnobotanical and Floristic studies in Western Nigeria" Lagos, Nigeria: The Organization of African Unity's Scientific Technical and   Research Commission, pp293-294.

Adjanohoun, E.J., Ake Assit, L., Floret, J.J., Guinko, S., Koumaré M. et al. (1979). Médecine   traditionnelle (MT) et pharmacopée, contribution aux études ethnobotaniques et floristiques   au Mali. ACCT. Paris; 27, 33 p.

African Pharmacopoeia Vol. 1 (1985). 2nd edition, Lagos, published by Organization of African   Unity's   Scientific, Technical and Research Commission, Lagos, Nigeria, pp3-4

Agbovie, T., Amponsah, K., Crentsil, O.R., Dennis, F., Odamtten, G.T. et al. (2002). Conservation   and sustainable use of medicinal plants in Ghana - Ethnobotanical Survey

Agyare, C., Asase, A., Lechtenberg, M., Niehues, M. et al. (2009). An ethnopharmacological survey and in vitro confirmation of ethnopharmacological use of medicinal plants used for wound healing in Bosomtwi-Atwima-Kwanwoma area, Ghana. Journal of Ethnopharmacology 125:393–403.

Ajaiyeoba, E.O., Falade, C.O., Fawole, O.I., Akinboye, D. et al., (2004). Efficacy of herbal remedies used by herbalists in Oyo State Nigeria for treatment of Plasmodium falciparum infections--a survey and an observation. African J Med Sci., 33(2):115-119

Ake Assi, L., (2001-2002). Flore de la Côte d'Ivoire: catalogue systématique, biogéographie et écologie. Mémoire de botanique systématique. Conservatoire et Jardin Botanique de Genève, 2 volumes.

Ake´ Assi, L., Guinko, S. (1986). Plants Used in Traditional Medicine in West Africa; Editions Roche: Basel

Akendengue, B., Lemamy, G.J., Bourobou, H.B., Laurens, A. (2005). Bioactive natural compounds from medico-magic plants of Bantu area. Studies in Natural Product Chemistry 32(12):803- 820.

Akisanya, A., Bevan, C.W.L., Hirst, J. (1959). West African timbers. II. Heartwood constituents of the genus Pterocarpus. Journal of the Chemical Society 2679-2681.

Alarcon-Aguilar, F.J., Zamilpa, A., Perez-Garcia, M.D., Almanza-Perez, J.C. et al., (2007). Effect of Hibiscus sabdariffa on obesity in MSG mice. Journal of Ethnopharmacology 114: 66-71.

Ajay, M., Chai, H.J., Mustafa, A.M., Gilani, A.H., Mustafa, M.R. (2007). Mechanisms of the antihypertensive effect of Hibiscus sabdariffa L. calyces. Journal of Ethnopharmacology 109:388393.

Amer, M.M. and Court, W.E. (1980). Leaf alkaloids of Rauwolfia vomitoria. Phytochemistry 19:1833-1836

Androulakis, X.M., Muga, S.J., Chen, F., Koita, Y. et al. (2006). Chemopreventive effects of Khaya senegalensis bark extract on human colorectal cancer. Anticancer Research 26(3B):2397-405

Anton, R., Haag-Berriere, M. (1980). The therapeutic uses of natural authraquinones other than laxative actions. Pharmacology suppliments 20:104-112

Apori, S.O., Castro, F.B., Shand, W.J., Orskov, E.R. (1998). Chemical composition, in sacco degradation and in vitro gas production of some Ghanaian browse plants. Animal Feed Science and Technology 76(1-2):129-138

Asase, A., Akweteya, G.A., Achelb, D.G. (2010). Ethnopharmacological use of herbal remedies for the treatment of malaria in the Dangme West District of Ghana. Journal of Ethnopharmacology 129:367–376.

Ashidi, J.S., Houghton, P.J., Hylands P.J., Efferth, T., (2010). Ethnobotanical survey and cytotoxicity testing of plants of South-western Nigeria used to treat cancer, with isolation of cytotoxic constituents from Cajanus cajan Millsp. Leaves. Journal of Ethnopharmacology 128:501– 512.

Asprey, G.F., Thornton, P. (1955). Medicinal Plants of Jamaica.III, West Indian Medical Journal 4:69-82

Asuzu, I.U., Anaga, A.O. (1991). Pharmacological screening of the aqueous extract of Alstonia boonei stem bark. Fitoterapia 63:411-417

Arthan, D., Kittakoop, P., Esen, A., Svasti, J. (2006). Furostanol glycoside 26-O-betaglucosidase from the leaves of Solanum torvum. Phytochemistry 67(1):27-33

Aweke, Getachew, Tapapul, Suzanne, (2005). Lawsonia inermis L. [Internet] Fiche de Protabase. Jansen,

P.C.M. & Cardon, D. (Editeurs). PROTA (Plant Resources of Tropical Africa / Ressources végétales de l'Afrique tropicale), Wageningen, Pays Bas. http://database.prota.org/recherche.htm. Visité le 24 juin.

Ayisi, N. K., Nyadedzor, C. (2003). Comparative in vitro effects of AZT and extracts of Ocimum gratissimum, Ficus polita, Clausena anisata, Alchornea cordifolia, and Elaeophorbia drupifera against HIV-1 and HIV-2 infections. Antiviral Research 58:25-33.

Balde, M.A. (1990). in Biological and Phytochemical Investigations on three plants widely used in Guinean traditional medicine. Doctoral Thesis Pharmaceutical Sciences. University of Antwerp, Belgium.

Balde, A.M., Apers, S., De Bruyne, T., Van Den Heuvel, H. et al. (2000). Steroids from Harrisonia abyssinica.; Planta Medica 66:67-69.

Balde, A.M., Apers, S., Claeys, M., Pieters, L., Vlietinck, A.J. (2001). Cycloabyssinone, a new cycloterpene from Harrisonia abyssinica. Fitoterapia 72:438-440.

Barbosa, L.C.D.A., Demuner, M.L.F.A.J., Pereira, A.A.D.S.C. (2001). Preparation and Phytotoxicity of sorgoleone analogues. Química Nova 24 (6).

Basilevskaia, (1969). Plantes Médicinales de Guinée ; Imprimerie Nationale Patrice Lumumba, Conakry ; 271 p. Conakry, République de Guinée.

Belemtougri, R.G., Constantin, B., Cognard, C., Raymond, G., Sawadogo, L. (2001). Effects of Sclerocarya birrea (A. rich) hochst (anacardiaceae) leaf extracts on calcium signalling in cultured rat skeletal muscle cells. Journal of Ethnopharmacology 76(3):247-252.

Bernard, B. (2001). Dictionnaire des plantes médicinales du monde ; Réalité et Croyance; Edition Estem ; 275 p.

Bennet, H. (1950). Alchornea cordifolia leaves and bark from Nigeria. Colonial plant annual Products 1:132-134.

Betti, J.L. (2004). An ethnobotanical study of medicinal plants among Pigmies in Dja biosphere Reserve, Cameroon. Afican Study Monographs 25(1):1-27.

Bevan, C.W.L., Ekong, D.E.U., Obasi, M.E., Powell, J.W. (1966). West African timbers. XIII. Extracts from the heartwood of Amphimas pterocarpoides and Pterocarpus erinaceus. Journal of the Chemical Society [Section] C: Organic (5):509-510.

Bierer, D.E., Fort, D.M., Mendez, C.D. et al., (1998). Ethnobotanical-directed discovery of the antihyperglycaemic properties of cryptolepine: its isolation from Cryptolepis sanguinolenta, synthesis, and in vitro and in vivo activities. Journal of Medicinal Chemistry, 41: 894-901

Blanco, M.M., Costa, C.A.R.A., Freire, A.O., Santos Jr, J.G. et al., (2007). Neurobehavioral effect of essential oil of Cymbopogon citratus in mice. Phytomedicine, 4: 007

Boullard, B. (2001). Dictionnaire des plantes médicinales du monde. Réalités et croyances. 25, 113, 249, 357, 374, 532 p.

Bouquet, A., Debray, M. (1974). Plantes médicinales de la Côte d'Ivoire.Travaux et Documents de l'ORSTOM., Paris, n 32, 232 p.

Boye, G.L. (1989). Studies on antimalarial action of Cryptolepis sanguinolenta extract. Proceedings of the International Symposium on East-West Medicine; Seoul, Korea, 243-51

Braca, A., Politi, M., Sanogo, R., Sanou, H, Morelli, I. et al. (2003). The Chemical Composition and Antioxidant Activity of Phenolic Compounds from Wild and Cultivated Sclerocarya birrea (Anacardiaceae) Leaves. Journal of Agricultural and Food Chemistry (51):66898-6695

British Pharmaceutical Codex (1949).

British Pharmaceutical Codex (1923).

Burkill, H.M (1995). The Useful Plants of West Tropical Africa Vol. 3 Family J-L Kew: Royal Botanic Garden. pp. 492-493.

Burkill, H. M. (1985). The Useful Plants of West Tropical Africa. 2nd Edition. Vol. 1. Royal Botanic Gardens, Kew. London

Carlini, E.A., Contar, J.P., Silva-Filho, A.R., Da Silveira-Filho, N.G. et al., (1986). Pharmacology of lemongrass (Cymbopogon citratus Stapf.) I: Effect of teas prepared from the leaves on laboratory Animals. Journal of Ethnopharmacology 17:37-64

Chabbra, S.C., Uiso, F.C., Mshiu, E.N. (1984). Phytochemical screening of Tanzanian medicinal plants. I. Journal of Ethnopharmacology 11(2):157-179.

Cheng, Z.H., Yu, B.Y., Yang, X.W. (2002). 27Nor triterpenoid glycosides from Mitragyna inermis. Phytochemistry 61:379-382

Chevallier, A. (1996). The Encyclopedia of Medicinal Plants. Printed by New Interlitho, Milan, Italy.

Chhabra, S.C., Uiso, F.C., (1991). Antibacterial activity of some Tanzanian plants used in traditional medicine. Fitoterapia 62:499–503

Chin, W.Y. (2002). A Guide to Medicinal Plants. Singapore Science Centre, Singapore.

Chukwujekwu, J.C., Coombes, P.H., Mulholland, D.A., van Staden, J. (2006). Emodin, an antibacterial anthraquinone from the roots of Cassia occidentalis. South African Journal of Botany 72, 295-297.

Chukwujekwu, J.C., van Staden, J., Smith, P. (2005).

Antibacterial, anti-inflammatory and antimalarial activities of some Nigerian medicinal plants. South African Journal of Botany 71: 316325.

Cimanga, R.K., Tona, G.L., Mesia, G.K., Kambu, O.K., Bakana, D.P. et al., (2006). Bioassayguided isolation of antimalarial triterpenoid acids from the leaves of Morinda lucida. Pharmaceutical Biology 44:677–681

Cimanga, K., Ying L., de Bruyne T., Apers S., Cos P., et al. (2001). Radical scavenging and xanthine oxidase inhibitory activity of phenolic compounds from Bridelia ferruginea stem bark. Journal of Pharmacy and Pharmacology 53:5:757-761.

Comley, J.C.W. (1990). New macrofilaricidal leads from plants?; Tropical Medical Parasitology 41(1):1-9.

Cook, J. A., Vanderjagt, D.J., Pastuszyn, A., Mounkaïla, G. et al. (1998). Nutrient content of two indigenous Plant foods of the werstern Sahel: Balanites aegyptiaca and Maerua crassifolia. Journal of Food Composition and Analysis 11:221-230.

Corzo-Martínez, M., Corzo, N., Villamiel, M. (2007). Biological properties of onions and garlic. Trends in Food Science and Technology 18: 609625.

Costa, C., Bortazzo, A., Allegri, G., Curcuroto, D., Traloli, P. (1992). Indole alkaloids from the roots on an African plant, Securidaca longependuculata. Isolation by column chromatography and preliminary structural characterization by mass spectrometry. Journal of heterocycle Chemestry. P:1641–1647

Costa-Campos, L., Iwu, M., Elisabetsky E., (2004). Lack of pro-convulsant activity of the antipsychotic alkaloid alstonine. Journal of Ethnopharmacology 93:307–310

Dalziel, J.M. (1936). The Useful Plants of West Tropical Africa London: Crown Agents for the Overseas

Governments and Administrations.

Dao, A. (1988). Etudes botaniques et phytochimiques de Sclerocarya birrea (A. Rich). Hochst.   (Anacardiaceae), Thèse de pharmacie, Bamako (Mali), N38, 69 p.

Diallo, M.S.T. (2004). Investigations ethnobotanique et phytochimique de Hymenocardia acida et   Lantana camara. Thèse de DEA de Phytothérapie et Plantes Médicinales, Département   Pharmacie, Faculté de Médecine pharmacie universite conakry

Diallo, M.S.T. (2002). Contribution à l'étude phytochimique de Hymenocardia acida Tull. 57 p thèse   de fin d'étude supérieure en Pharmacie; Faculté de Médecine Pharmacie-Odonto Stomatologie, Université de Conakry

Diehl, M.S., Kamanzi Atindehou, K., Téré, H., Betschart, B. (2004). Prospect for anthelminthic plants in the Ivory Coast using ethnobotanical criteria. Journal of Ethnopharmacology 95:277– 284.

Duke, J.A., Atchley, A.A. (1986). Handbook of proximate analysis tables of higher plants. Boca Raton, USA: C R C Press. p36.

Duke, J.A., wain, K.K. (1981).The medical plants of the world. Computer index with more than 85000 entries, Vol 3.

Duke, J.A. (1985). Handbook of medicinal herbs. Boca Raton, USA: CRC Press.

Durodola, J.I. (1977). Antibacterial property of crude extracts from a herbal wound healing remedy-   Ageratum conyzoides, L. Planta Medica 32(4):388-390

Durodola, J.I. (1974). Antineoplastic property of a crystalline compound extracted from Morinda   lucida. Planta Medica 26:208–211

Dwuma-Badu, D., Ayim, J.S.K., Fiagbe, N.Y.I., Knapp, P.E.

et al., (1978). Constituents of West African medicinal plants XX: Quindoline from Cryptolepis sanguinolenta. Journal of Pharmaceutical Science 67:4339-434

Ejoh, A.R., Tanya, A.N., Djuikwo, N.V., Mbofung, C.M. (2005a). Effect of processing and preservation methods on vitamin c and total carotenoid levels of some Vernonia (bitter leaf) species African Journal of Food and Nutritional Sciences 5(2):1-11.

Ejoh, R.A., Tanya, A.N., Djuikwo, V.N., Mbofung, C.M. (2005b). Effect of processing and preservation on the iron and vitamin A (total carotenoid) levels of some species of Vernonia. Sciences des Aliments 25(3):185-192.

El- Said, F., Sofowora, E. A., Malcom, S.A, Hofer, A. (1969). An investigation into the efficacy of Ocimum gratissimum as used in Nigerian native medicine. Planta Medica 17(2):195-200.

Elujoba, A.A., Olawode, E.O. (2004). Technical Report of the commissioned chromatographic fingerprint analysis on Allium sativum bulb to World Health Organization, Nigeria.

Elujoba, A. A., Ogunti, E.O. (1993). Pharmacopoeial and biological standardization of Cassia alata and Cassia podocarpa with reference to Senna. Glimpses in Plant Research XI, 469-479.

Elujoba, A.A., Ajulo, O.O., Iweibo, G.O. (1989). Chemical and Biological analyses of Nigerian

Eromosele, I.C., Eromosele, C.O., Kuzhkuzha, D.M. (1991). Evaluation of mineral elements and ascorbic acid contents in fruits of some wild plants. Plant Foods and Human Nutrition 41(2):151-154.

Esser, K.B., Semagn, K., Wolde Yohannes, L. (2003). Medicinal use and social status of the soap berry endod (Phytolacca dodecandra) in Ethiopia. Journal of Ethnopharmacology 85(2–3):269–277.

Evans, W.C. (1996). Trease and Evans' Pharmacognosy (14th Edition). WB Saunders Co. Ltd.   London. pp 336.

Faizi, S., Siddiqui, B.S., Saleem, R., Siddiqui, S., Aftab, K., Giliani, A.H. (1994). Isolation and   structure elucidation of new nitrile and mustard oil glycosides from Moringa oleifera and their   effect on blood pressure. Journal of natural Products 57:1256-1261.

Fatima, N., Tapondjou, L.A., Lontsi, D., Sondengam, B.L. et al. (2002). Quinovic acid glycosides   from   Mitragyna stipulosa-first examples of natural inhibitors of snake venom   Phosphodiesterase i. Natural Product Letters 16(6):389-393

Freire, S.M.F., Emim, A.J.S., Lapa, A.J., Souccar, C. et al. (1993). Analgesic and anti- inflammatory   properties of Scoparia dulcis L. extract and glutinol in rodents. Phytotherapy Research 7:408-   414.

Galvez, J., Zarzuelo, A., Busson, R., Cobbaert, C., De Witte, P. (1992). (-)-Epicatechin-3-galloyl   ester: a secretagogue compound from the bark of Sclerocarya birrea. Planta Medica   58(2):174175.

Gaiwe, R., Nkulinkiye-Nfura, T., Bassenne, E., Olschwan, G., Ba, D. et al. (1989). Calcium et mucilage dans les feuilles de Adansonia digitata (Baobab). Pharmaceutical Biology   27(2):101-104

Gazzaneo, L.R.S., Paiva de Lucena, R.F., Paulino de Albuquerque, U. (2005). Knowledge and use of medicinal plants by local specialists in a region of Atlantic Forest in the state of Pernambuco   (Northeastern Brazil). Journal of Ethnobiology and Ethnomedicine 1:9.

Gellert, E., Raymond-Hamet, Schlittler, E. (1951). Die Konstitution des Alkaloids Cryptolepin. (The   structure of the alkaloid cryptolepine) Helvetica Chimica Acta; 34: 642-51.

Ghana Herbal Pharmacopoeia (1992). The Advent Press: Accra, Ghana

Gill, S. (1978). Flavonoid compounds of the Ageratum conyzoides L. herb. Acta Poloniae Pharmaceutica 35(2):241-243.

Gill, L. S. (1992). Ethnomedical Uses of Plants in Nigeria. Printed and Published by University of Benin Press. Benin-City, Nigeria

Glasby, J.S. (1991). Dictionary of Plants Containing Secondary Metabolites. Taylor & Francis, London 488

Godding, E. W. (1998). Laxatives and the special roles of Senna. Pharmacology 36(1):230-236

Gorman, R., Schreiber, L., Kolodziej, H. (2004). Cuticular wax profiles of leaves of some traditionally used African Bignoniaceae. Zeitschrift für Naturforschung: C. 59(9-10):631635.

Grieve, M. (1984).A Modern Herbal, Penguin. ISBN 0-14-046-440-9

Gupta, D. (1991).Flavonoid glycosides from Cassia alata. Phytochemistry 30(8): 2761-2763

Gupta, S., Pradeep, S., Soni, P.L. (2005). Chemical modification of Cassia occidentalis seed gum: carbamoylethylation. Carbohydrate Polymers 59:501–506.

Haensel, R., Keller, K., Rimpler, H., Schneider, G. (1994). Hagers Handbuch der Pharm.Praxis 5.Auflage Springer Heidelberg, New York Band 4: 135-37.

Haji-Faraji, M., Haji-Tarkhani, A. (1999). The effect of sour tea (Hibiscus sabdariffa) on essential hypertension. Journal of Ethnopharmacology 65:231–236

Haidara, T. (1999). Etude botanique, phytochimique et

pharmacologique de trios plantes de la   pharmacopée malienne indiquées dans le traitement du diabète, Thèse Pharmacie, FMPOS,   Université de Bamako, Mali.

Hashem, F.M., Haggag M.Y., Galal, A.M.S. (1980). A phytochemical study of Carica papaya L.   growing in Egypt. Egyptian Journal of Pharmaceutical Sciences 21 (3/4):199-214.

Hassanali, A., Bentley, M.D., Slawin, A.M.Z., Williams, D.J. et al. (1987). Pedonin, a spiro   tetranortriterpenoid   insect antifeedant from Harrisonia abyssinica. Phytochemistry 26(2) 573575.

Hayashi, T. (2000). Biologically active diterpenoids from Scoparia dulcis (scrophulariaceae). Studies   in   Natural Product Chemistry 21(2):689-727.

Hentchoya, H.J. (1991). Contribution a l'etude de plantes medecinales du Cameroun; Raport sur la   prospection et la selection de quelques plantes devant faire l'objet d'une etude chimique.

Hosny, M., Khalifa, T., Caliş, I., Wright, A.D., Sticher, O. (1992). Balanitoside, a furostanol   glycoside, and 6-methyldiosgenin from Balanites aegyptiaca. Phytochemistry, 31(10):3565-   3569

Hutchings, A., Haxton Scott, A., Lewis, G., Cunningham, A. (1996). Zulu Medicinal Plants/An   Inventory. University of Natal Press, Pietermaritzburg

Igoli, O.J., Gray, I.A. (2008). Friedelanone and other triterpenoids from Hymenocardia acida. International   Journal of Physical Sciences 3(6)156-158.

Inngjerdingen, K., Nergård, C.S., Diallo, D., Mounkoro, P.P., Paulsen, B.S. (2004). An   ethnopharmacological survey of plants used for wound healing in Dogonland, Mali, West Africa. Journal of Ethnopharmacology 92:233–244.

Irobi, O.N., Moo-Young, M., Anderson, W.A., Daramola, S.O. (1994). Antimicrobial activity of bark extracts of Bridelia ferruginea (Euphorbiaceae). Journal of Ethnopharmacology 43(3):185- 190

Irvine, F.R. (1961). Woody Plants of Ghana with Special Reference to their Uses London: Oxford University Press, pp 40-520

Iwu, M.M. (1993). In: Handbook of African Medicinal Plants. CRC Press, Boca Raton, FL. pp 116- 118

Iwu, M.M. (1993). Handbook of African Medicinal Plants. Boca Raton, FL, CRC Press Inc., pp. 219– 220.

Iwu, M.M. and Court, W.E. (1982). Stem bark alkaloids of Rauwolfia vomitoria. Planta Medica 45, 105-111

Hatano, T., Mizuta, S., Ito, H., Yoshida, T. (1999). C-Glycosidic flavonoids from Cassia occidentalis. Phytochemistry 52:1379-1383.

Hauptman, H., Lacerda, V.L. (1950). Journal of American Chemical Society 72: 1492

Hotellier, F., Delaveau, P., Poussett, J.I. (1981). Naucleofoline, a new alkaloid from Nauclea latifolia SM (Rubiacea). C.R. Seances Acad. Sci. Ser. 2 293(8):577-578

Hutchinson, J., Dalziel, J.M. (1958). Flora of West Tropical Africa 2nd Edition, Revised by Keay R. W. J London: Crown Agents for Overseas Governments and Administration. p. 476.

Ikram, M., Hussain, S.F. (1978). Compendium of Medicinal Plants. Pakistan Council of Scientific and Industrial Research, Peshawar 77-78.

Kala, C. P. (2005). Ethnomedicinal botany of the Apatani in the Eastern Himalayan region of India. Journal of Ethnobiology and Ethnomedicine 1:11

Kamel, M.S. (1998). A Furostanol saponin from fruits of

Balanites aegyptiaca. Phytochemistry   148(4):755-757.

Kambizi, L., Afolayan, A.J. (2001). An ethnobotanical study of plants used for the treatment of   sexually   transmitted diseases (njovhera) in Guruve District, Zimbabwe. Journal of Ethnopharmacology 77: 5–9.

Karou, D., Mamoudou, H., Dicko, S.S., Jacques, S.,Traore, A.S. (2003). Antimalarial activity of Sida   acuta Burm. f. (Malvaceae) and Pterocarpus erinaceus Poir. (Fabaceae). Journal of   Ethnopharmacology 89:291–294

Kerharo, J., Bouquet, A. (1950). Plantes médi

cinales et toxiques de la Côte d'Ivoire, Haute Volta, Edition Vigot, 67

Kerharo, J., Adam, J.G. (1974). La pharmacopée Sénégalaise traditionnelle, plantes médicinales et   toxiques.   Vigot, Paris, p. 241-245

Khan, M.R., Ndaalio, G., Nkunya, M.H.H, Wevers, H. (1978). Studies on the rationale of African   traditional   medicine Part II. Preliminary screening of medicinal plants for antigonococci activity, Pak., J. SCI. IND. RES. 27(516):189192.

Kitisin, T. (1952). Pharmacological studies III Phyllanthus niruri. Siriraj Hospital Gaz 4:641649.

Kirira, P.G., Rukunga, G.M., Wanyonyi, A.W., Muregi, F.M. et al. (2006). Anti-plasmodial activity   and   toxicity   of extracts of plants used in traditional malaria therapy in Meru and kilifi   Districts   of   Kenya.   Journal   of Ethnopharmacology 106(3):403-407

Kohler, I., Jenett Siems, K., Kraft, C., Siems, K. et al. (2002). Herbal remedies traditionally used   against   malaria   in Ghana: bioassay-guided fractionation of Microglossa pyridolia   (Asteraceae) Z Naturforsch ser C 57C (11/12):1022-1027.

Koumaglo, K., Gbeassor, M., Nikabu, O., De Souza, C., Werner, W. (1992). Effects of three compounds extracted from Morinda lucida. Planta Medica. 58:533–534

Kumaresan, A., Mshella, T.A., Aliu, Y.O. (1984). Biochemical evaluation of bagawura seeds for use as livestock feed. Animal Feed Science and Technology 11:45-48

Kusirisin, W., Jaikang, C., Chaiyasut, C., Narongchai, P. (2009). Effect of Polyphenolic Compounds from Solanum torvum on Plasma Lipid Peroxidation, Superoxide anion and Cytochrome P450 2E1 in Human Liver Microsomes. Medicinal Chemistry 5:583-588.

Irvine, F. R. (1961). Woody Plants of Ghana. Oxford University Press.

Irvin, F.R. (1961). in Wood plants of Ghana ; London : Oxford University Press, pp739-740. Lisowski, S. (2009). Flore (Angiospermes) de la République de Guinée ; première partie (texte). Scripta Botanica Belgica, 41, 517p

Lans, C., (2007b). Ethnomedicines used in Trinidad and Tobago for reproductive problems. Journal of Ethnobiology and Ethnomedicine 3:13

Laurens, A. (1976). Sur des Anacardiacées africaines et malgaches, Poupartia birrea, Pourpartia caffra et Anacardium occidentale (Etude particulière des polyphénols des feuilles), Thèse doctorat, Pharm. (Etat), Paris

Lemma, A., Brody, G., Newell, G.W., Parkhurst R.M.,Skinner, W.A. (1972). Endod (Phytolacca dodecandra), a natural product molluscicide: increased potency with butanol extraction. The Journal of Parasitology 1972; 58: 104-107

Liu, J.Y., Chen, C.C., Wang, W.H., Hsu, J.D., Yang, M.Y. et al.,(2006). The protective effects of Hibiscus sabdariffa extract on CCl4-induced liver fibrosis in rats. Food and Chemical Toxicology, 44.

Lockett, C.T., Calvert, C.C. and Grivetti, L.E. (2000). Energy and micronutrient composition of   dietary and medicinal wild plants consumed during drought. Study of rural Fulani,   Northeastern Nigeria. International Journal of Food Science and Nutrition 51:195-208

Loua, J. (2004). Investigations thérapeutiques et phytochimique de Lawsonia inermis L. utilisé en   médecine traditionnelle guinéenne dans le traitement du paludisme ; thèse de Phytothérapie et   Plantes Médicinales, Département de Pharmacie, Faculté de médecine-   PharmacieOdontostomatologie, Université de Conakry, Guinée

Luziatelli, G., Sørensen, M., Theilade, I., Mølgaard P. (2010). Asháninka medicinal plants: a case   study from the native community of Bajo Quimiriki, Junín, Peru. Journal of Ethnobiology and   Ethnomedicine 6: 21

Magassouba, F.B., Diallo, A., Kouyaté, M., Mara, F., et al., (2007). Ethnobotanical survey and   antibacterial activity of some plants used in Guinean traditional medicine. Journal of   Ethnopharmacology 114:44-53.

Mahmood, N., Moore, P.S., De Tommasi, N., De Simone, F., Colman, S. et al. (1993). Inhibition of   HIV   infection   by caffeoylquinic acid derivates. Antiviral Chemistry and Chemotherapy. 4:235240.

Mbosso, E.J., Ngouela, S., Nguedia, J.C., Penlap, V., Rohmer, M., Tsamo, E. (2008). Spathoside, a   cerebroside and other antibacterial constituents of the stem bark of Spathodea campanulata.   Natural Product Research 22(4):296-304.

Mehmood, S., Orhan, I., Ahsan, Z., Aslan, S. et al. (2008). Fatty acid composition of seed oil of   different   Sorghum bicolor   varieties,   Food   Chemistry   (2008),   doi: 0.1016/j.foodchem.2008.01.014.

Mensah A Y, Houghton P J, Fleischer T C, Adu C, Agyare C, Ameade A E. (2003). Antimicrobial   and   antioxidant properties of two Ghanaian plants used traditionally for wound healing. Journal of Pharmacy and Pharmacology 55(Supplement):S-4.

Mesia, G.K., Tona, T.H., Nanga, T.H., Cimanga, R.K., Apers, S. et al. (2008). Antiprotozoal and cytotoxic screening of 45 plant extracts from Democratic Republic of Congo. Journal of Ethnopharmacology 115:409-415.

Milt, S., Bone, K. (2001). Principles and Practice of Phytotherapy, Modern Herbal Medicine. Churchill Livingstone, London. pp. 394 to 403

Mlambo, V., Mould, F.L, Sikosana, J.L.N., Smith, T. et al., (2008). Chemical composition and in vitro fermentation of tannin-rich tree fruits. Animal Feed Science and Technology, 140; 402–417

Moneret Vautrin, D.A., Benoist, M., Laxenaire, M.C., Croizier, A., Gueant, J.L. (1985). Allergy to chymopapain: value of predictive tests before chemonucleolysis. Annals French Anesth Reanim 4(3):313-3 15.

Morton, J.F. (1981). Atlas of medicinal plants of middle America: Bahamas to Yucatan. CC Thomas, springfield, II.

Mpiana, P., Tshibangu, D., Shetonde, O., Ngbolua, K. (2007). In vitro antidrepanocytary actvity (anti-sickle cell anemia) of some Congolese plants ; 14(2):192-195.

Mshana, N.R., Abbiw, D.K., Addae-Mensah, I., Ahiyi, M.R.A., Ekper, J.A., et al., (2000). Traditional medicine and pharmacopoeia. Contribution to the revision of Ethnobotanical and Floristics Studies of Ghana. Organisation of African Unity/Scientific, technical and research committee.

Muluvi, G.M., Sprent, J.I., Soranzo, N., Provan, J., Odee, D. et al. (1999). Amplified fragment length polymorphism (AFLP) analysis of genetic variation in Moringa oleifera Lam.

Molecular   Ecology, 8:463-470.

Murakami, A., Kitazono, Y., Jiwajinda, S., Koshimizu, K., Ohigashi, H. (1998). Niaziminin, a   thiocarbamate from the leaves of Moringa oleifera, holds a strict structural requirement for inhibition   of   tumor-promoter-induced EpsteinBarr virus activation. Planta Medica 64:319-323

Muthu, C., Ayyanar, M., Raja, N., Ignacimuthu, S. (2006). Medicinal plants used by traditional   healers   in Kancheepuram District of Tamil Nadu

Nahrstedt, A. (1987). Recent developments in chemistry, distribution and biology the cyanogenic glycosides.   In: Hostettmann, K., Lea, P.J. (Eds). Biologically active natural products. Oxford,   USA: Oxford Science Publications, p167184, 213-234.

Nath, M.C. (1945). The new antidiabetic principle (amellin) occurring in nature. I. Studies on some of   its biochemical properties. Chemical Abstracts 39:3361-3362

Nath, D., Sethi, N., Singh, R.K., Jain, A.K. (1992). Commonly used Indian arbortifacient plants with   special reference to their teratologic effects in rats. Journal of Ethnopharmacology 36: 147-   154.

Newall, C. A., Anderson, A.L et al. (1996). Herbal medicines: a guide for health - care professionals.

Njorege, G.N., Bussman, R.W. (2006). Traditional management of ear, nose and thorat (ENT)   diseases   in central Kenya. Journal of Ethnobotany and Ethnomedicine 2(1): 54. London,   Pharmaceutical Press

Nigeria Herbal Pharmacopoeia (2008). The Federal Secretariat Complex, Abuja, Nigeria

Niyonzima, G. (1997). Contribution to the study of the antidiabetic activity of an African medicinal   plant: Spathodea camapanulata P. Beauv. (Bignoniaceae). Thesis,

University of Antwerp   (Belgium

Nour, A.A.A.M., Ahmed, A.H.R., Abdel-Gayoum, A.G.A.A. (1986). chemical study of Balanites   aegyptiaca L. (Lalob) fruits grown in Sudan. Journal of Science of Food and Agriculture 36   :1254–1258

Noumi, E., Houngue, F., Lontsi, D. (1999). Traditional medicines in prymary health care: plants used   for   the treatment of hypertension in Bafia Cameroon. Fitoterapia 70(2):134–139

Nuhu, A. M., Mshelia, M.S., Yakubu, Y. (2000). Antimicrobial screening of the bark extract of   Pterocarpus erinaceus tree. Journal of Chemical Society of Nigeria 25:85-87

Odebiyi, O.O. (1978). Preliminary phytochemical and antimicrobial examination of leaves of   Securidaca longepedunculata. Nigerian Journal of Pharmaceutics 9:29-30

Odeleye, O.M. (2004). Comparative Pharmacognostical studies on Aloe schwenfurthii Baker and   Aloe   vera (Linn.) Burm. F." M. Sc (Pharmacognosy) Thesis, Obafemi Awolowo University,   Nigeria

Ogunti, E.O., Elujoba, A.A. (1993). Laxative activity of Cassia alata. Fitoterapia 64 (5):437– 439.

Ogunti, E.O., Aladesanmi, J.A., Adesanya, S.A, (1991). Antibacterial activity of Cassia alata.   Fitoterapia 62:537

Ojewole, J.A.O. (1984). Studies on the pharmacology of echitamine, an alkaloid from the stem bark   of   Alstonia boonei L. (Apocynaceae). International Journal of Crude Drug Research 22:121-   143

Ojewole, J.A. (2003). Hypoglycemic effect of Sclerocarya birrea [(A. Rich.) Hochst.]   [Anacardiaceae]   stem-bark aqueous extract in rats. Phytomedicine, 10(8):675-681.

Ojewole, J.A., Mawoza, T., Chiwororo, W.D., Owira, P.M. (2010). Sclerocarya birrea (A. Rich) Hochst. ['Marula'] (Anacardiaceae): a review of its phytochemistry, pharmacology and toxicology and its ethnomedicinal uses. Phytotherapy Research 24(5):633-639.

Okafor J.I, Eze E.A., Njoku O. U. (2001). Nigerian Journal of Natural Products and Medicine 5 59- 60.

Okorie, D.A. (1982). Chromones and Limonoids from Harrisonia abyssinica. Phytochemistry 21: 2424-2426
Rajab, M.S., Rugutt, J.K., Fronczek, F.R., Fischer, N.H. (1997). Structural revision of Harrisonin and 12-Beta-Acetoxyharrisonin, two limonoids from Harrisonia abyssinica. Journal of Natural Products 60(8):822-825.

Okpekon, T., Yolou, S., Gleye, C., Roblot, F. et al. (2004). Antiparasitic activities of medicinal plants used in Ivory Coast. Journal of Ethnopharmacology 90:91-97.

Oladiji, A.T., Jacob, T.O., Yakubu, M.T. (2007). Anti-anaemic potentials of aqueous extract of Sorghum bicolor (L.) moench stem bark in rats. Journal of Ethnopharmacology 111:651-656

Olaniyi A. A., Marquis V. O. (1975). Phytochemical and preliminary Pharmacological investigation of an alkaloid obtained from Momordica foetida, Journal of Pharmacy, 6: 117119

Oliver, B. (1959). Nigerian Medicinal Plants. The Nigerian College of Science and Technology, Ibadan. Nigeria (1959) pp. 60-63

Oliver-Bever, B. (1960). Medicinal Plants of Nigeria. Nigerian College of Arts, Science and Technology, p. 20

Oliver-Bever, B.E.P. (1986). Medicinal Plants in Tropical West Africa. Cambridge: Cambridge University Press; pgs 18, 41, 131, 205

Olowokudejo, J.D., Kadiri, A.B., Travih, V.A. (2008). An

Ethnobotanical Survey of Herbal Markets and Medicinal Plants in Lagos State of Nigeria. Ethnobotanical Leaflets 12: 851-865.

Onabanjo, A.O., Agbaje, E.O., Odusote, O.O. (1993). Effects of Aqueous Extracts of Cymbopogon citratus in Malaria. Journal of Protozoological Research 3:40–45

Onajobi, F.D. (1986). Smooth muscle contracting lipid-soluble principles in chromatographic fractions of Ocimum gratissimum. Journal of Ethnopharmacology,18:3-11.

Oyen, L.P.A. (2008). Tinospora bakis (A.Rich.) Miers. In: Schmelzer, G.H. & Gurib-Fakim, A. (Editeurs). Prota 11(1): Medicinal plants/Plantes médicinales 1. [CD-Rom]. PROTA, Wageningen, Pays Bas.

Pai, M., Marchand, J., Ratle, G., FrançoisJarreau, J. (1968). L'Hymenocardine, alcaloides de l'Hymenocardia acida Tull ; Bulletin de la Société Chimique de France, n 7.

Pankhurst, R. (1965). A historical examination of traditional Ethiopian medicine and surgery. Ethiopian Medical Journal, 3: 157-172.

Parkhurst, R.M., Thomas, D.W., Skinner, W.A., Cary, L.W. (1973). Molluscicidal saponins of Phytolacca dodecandra: oleanoglycotoxin-A. Phytochemistry 12: 1437-1442

Paris, R., Mignon, H. (1958). Sur quelques Méliaceae réputés fébrifuges. Bulletin Societe Pharmacologie 46:104-108

Paris, R. (1943). Sur une Apocynacee africaine, le Rauwolfia vomitoria. Annals of Pharmacy France 1:138-142.

Patel, V.K., Venkatakrishna-Bhatt, H. (1988). Folklore therapeutic indigenous plants in periodontal disorders in India (review, experimental and clinical approach). Internationa Journal of Clinical Pharmacology, Therapeutics and Toxicology 26(4):176-184.

Paulino de Albuquerque, U., Monteiro, J.M., Ramos, M.A., Cavalcanti de Amorim, E.L. (2007). Medicinal and magic plants from a public market in northeastern Brazil. Journal of Ethnopharmacology 110:76–91.

Pelissier, Y., Marion, C., Casadebaig, J., Milhau, M., Kone, D., et al., (1994). A Chemical, Bacteriological, Toxicological and Clinical Study of the Essential Oil of Lippia multiflora Mold (Verbenaceae) Journal of Essential Oil Research 6:623-630

Perry C.M (1980). Medicinal plants of East and Southeast Asia. MIT Press, Cambridge MA

Pérez-Amador, M.C., Muñoz, O.V., García, C.J.M., González, E.A.R. (2007). Alkaloids in Solanum torvum Sw (Solanaceae). International Journal of Experimental Botany 76:39-45. ISSN 0031- 9457

Phillipson, J.D., Wright, C.W. (1991). Can Ethnopharmacology contribute to the development of antimalarial agents? Journal of Ethnopharmacology 32:155-165.

Pradhan, B.K., Badola, H.K. (2008). Ethnomedicinal plant use by Lepcha tribe of Dzongu valley, bordering Khangchendzonga Biosphere Reserve, in North Sikkim, India. Journal of Ethnobiology and Ethnomedicine 4, 22.

Pruja, S. (1987). Contribution à l'étude phytochimique de Alchornea cordifolia mémoire de DEA INP Toulouse

Purwar, C., Rai, R., Srivastava, N., Singh, J. (2003). New flavonoid glycosides from Cassia occidentalis. Indian Journal of Chemistry Section B-Organic Chemistry Including Medicinal Chemistry 42:434-436

Rahman, W., Ilyas, M. (1961). Flavone glycosides from the flowers of Argemone mexicona L. (Papaveraceae). Comptes Rendus Hebdomadaires des Seances de 1 Academie des Sciences 27:252

Rajab, M.S., Fronczek, F.R., Mulholland, D.A., Rugutt, J.K. (1999). 11-Beta, 12- BetaDiacetoxyharrisonin, a tetranortriterpenoid from Harrisonia abyssinica. Phytochemistry 52(1): 127-133.

Rai, P.P., Abdullahi, N. (1978). Occurrence of anthraquinone in Cassia species. Nigerian Journal of Pharmacy 9:160–165.

Ramana, D.B.V., Singh, S., Solankia, K.R., Negi, A.S. (2000). Nutritive evaluation of some nitrogen and non-nitrogen-fixing multipurpose tree species. Animal Feed Science and Technology 88:103-111.

Rashid, M.A., Gustafson, K.R., Cardellina, J.H., Boyd, M.R. (2000). A new podophyllotoxin derivative from Bridelia ferruginea. Natural Product Letters 14(4): 285-292.

Rodrigues, E. (2006). Plants and Animals Utilized as Medicines in the Jaú National Park (JNP), Brazilian Amazon. Phytotherapy Research 20:378–391.

Sahu, T. R. (1984). Less known uses of weeds as medicinal plants. Ancient Science of Life.,3 (4): 245-249.

Sainsbury, M., Sofowora, E.A. (1971). Essential oil from the leaves and inflorescence of Ocimum gratissimum. Phytochemistry 10:3309

Samy, R.P., Ignacimuthu, S. (2000). Antibacterial activity of some folklore medicinal plants used by tribals in Western Ghats of India. Journal of Ethnopharmacology 69:63-71

Samy, R.P. (2005). Antimicrobial activity of some medicinal plants from India. Fitoterapia 76:697699.

Satyanarayana, K. (1969). Chemical examination of Scoparia dulcis (L): Part I. Journal of Indian Chemical Society 46:765-766.

Sawe, J.J., Tuitoek, J.K., Ottaro, J.M. (1998). Evaluation of common tree leaves or pods as supplements for goats on range area of Kenya. Small Ruminant Research 28:31–37.

Senatore, F., Formisano, C., Sanogo, R. (2004). Essential oil from aerial parts of Vernonia colorata drake and Vernonia nigritiana Oliver et Hiern. (Asteraceae) growing wild in Mali Journal of Essential Oil-Bearing Plants 7(3):267-274

Silva, O., Duarte, A., Cabrita, J., Pimentel, M., et al., (1996). Antimicrobial activity of GuineaBissau traditional remedies. Journal of Ethnopharmacology 50:55-59

Singh, S., Pandey, V.B., Singh, T.D. (2011). Alkaloids and flavonoids of Argemone mexicana. Natural Product Research 2011. [Epub ahead of print]

Singh, Y.N. (1986). Traditional medicine in Fiji. Some herbal folk cures used by Fiji Indians. Journal of ethnopharmacology 15(1):57-88

Sittie, A.A., Lemmich, B., Olsen, C.E., Hviid, I., Kharazmi, A. et al. (1999). Structure–Activity studies: in vitro antileishmanial and antimalarial activites of anthraquinones from Morinda lucida. Planta Medica 65:259–261.

Silvere, N., Barthelemy, N., Etienne, T., Beibam, L., Sondengam, J.D.C. (1990). Spathodic acid: A triterpene acid from the stem bark of Spathodea campanulata. Phytochemistry 29(12): 39593961.

Shellard, E.J., Sarpong, K. (1969). The alkaloids of the leaves of Mitragyna inermis (Willd.) O. Kuntze. Journal of Pharmacy and Pharmacology 21(suppl):113-117

Shellard, E.J., Sarpong, K. (1970). The alkaloids pattern in the leaves, stem-bark and root-bark of Mitragyna species from Ghana. Journal of Pharmacy and Pharmacology, 22 (Suppl.):34-39.

Shellard, E.J., Phillipson, J.D., Sarpong, K. (1971). Rhynchophylline and isorhynchophylline N- oxides from species of Mitragyna. Phytochemistry 10:2505-2511

Smith, G.C., Clegg, M.S., Keen, C.L., Grivetti, L.E. (1996). Mineral values of selected plant foods   common to southern Burkina Faso and to Niamey, Niger, West Africa. International Journal of Food Science and Nutrition 47(1):41-53

Suekawa, M., Ishige, A., Yuasa, K. et al., (1984). Pharmacological studies on ginger I.   Pharmacological actions of pungent constituents, (6)-gingerol and (6)-shogaol. Journal of   Pharmacobiodynamics 7:836-848

Tabuti, J.R.S., Lye, K.A., Dhillion, S.S. (2003). Traditional herbal drugs of Bulamogi, Uganda: plants,   use   and administration. Journal of Ethnopharmacology 88:19–44

Tang, C.S. (1971). Benzyl isothiocyanate of papaya fruit. Phytochemistry 10:117.

Tapondjou, L.A., Lontsi, D., Sondengam, B.L., Choudhary, M.I. et al. (2002). Structure-activity   relationship   of triterpenoids   isolated   from   Mitragyna   stipulosa   on cytotoxicity; Archives of   Pharmaceutical   Research 25(3): 270-274.

Telefo, P.B., Lienou, L.L., Yemele, M.D., Lemfack, M.C., Mouokeu, C. et al. (2011).   Ethnopharmacological survey of plants used for the treatment of female infertility in Baham,   Cameroon. Journal of Ethnopharmacology 136:178–187

Tona, L., Cimanga, R.K., Mesia, K., Musuamba, C.T. et al (2004). In vitro antiplasmodial activity of   extracts   and fractions from seven medicinal plants used in the Democratic Republic of Congo.   Journal of Ethnopharmacology 93:27-32

Trease, G.E., Evans, W.C. (1972). Pharmacognosy 13th edition, London: Bailliere Tindall

Tona, L., Kambu, K., Ngimbi, N., et al., (1998). Antiamoebic and phytochemical screening of some   Congolese   medicinal plants. Journal of Ethnopharmacology 61(1): 57-65

Toury, J., Lunven, P., Giorgi, R., Jacquesson, M. (1957). Extrait tiré dans le baobab, arbre providence de l'Afrique. Anale de la nutrition et de l'alimentation, In Ministere De L'economie Rurale- Direction Des Eaux Et Forêts, Leçon N 3, p. 1-4

Ukwe, C.V. (1997). Antiulcer activity of aqueous stembark extract of Hymenocardia acida Tul (Euphorbiaceae). International Journal of Pharmacognosy 35(5) 354-357.

Vonthron-Senecheau, C., Weniger, B., Ouattara, M., Bi, F.T. et al. (2003). In vitro antiplasmodial activity and cytotoxicity of ethnobotanically selected Ivorian plants; Journal of Ethnopharmacology 87:221-225.

Wallis, T. E. (1967). Textbook of Pharmacognosy" 5th Edition published by J and A Churchill Ltd, London.

Watt, J.M. (1962.) Leguminosae. In: J.M. Watt and M.G. Breyer-Brandwijk (Eds.), The Medicinal and Poisonous Plants of Southern and Eastern Africa. Livingstone Ltd., Edinburgh 546

Watt, J., Breyer-Brandwijk, M.C. (1962). The medicinal and poisonous plants of Southern and Eastern Africa, 2nd Ed. Livingstone, E.S. Publishers, Edinburgh

Weninger ,B., Rouzier, R.M., Henrys, D.D., Henrys, J.H., Anthon, R. (1986). Popular medicine of Plateau of Haiti. 2 Ethnopharmacological inventory. Journal of ethnopharmacology 17(1):13- 30

WHO monographs on selected medicinal plants (1999). Vol. 1, published by World Health Organization, Geneva. .

Wome, B. (1985). Recherches ethnopharmacognosiques sur les plantes médicinales utilisées en médecine traditionnelle à Kisangani (Haut-Zaïre).Thèse de doctorat, Université libre de Bruxelles, Fac. Sc., 561 p.

World Health Organization (1999). WHO Monographs on selected medicinal plants. Vol 1, published by WHO, Geneva

Yuan, T., Yang, S.P., Zhang, C.R., Zhang, S., Yue, J.M. (2009). Two limonoids, khayalenoids A and B with an unprecedented 8-oxatricyclo[4.3.2.0(2,7)]undecane motif, from Khaya senegalensis. Organic Letters 11(3):617-20.

Yuan-Yuan, L.U., Jian-Guang, L.U.O., Ling-Yi, K.O.N.G. (2011). Chemical Constituents from Solanum torvum. Chinese Journal of Natural Medicines 9(1):30–32

Zhang, H., Tan, J., Vanderveer, D., Wang, X., Wargovich, M.J., Chen, F. (2009). Khayanolides from African mahogany Khaya senegalensis (Meliaceae): A revision. Phytochemistry. 70(2):294-9.

ABOUT THE AUTHOR

Adamu Dede Murza Adamu Dede Murza is a graduate of Biology Education from the prestigious Ahnadu Bello University Zaria Nigeria. He is currently working with the Federal Ministry of Education in Nigeria as a biology teacher. The author is interested in reseach work related to uncovering medicinal uses and applications of plants tin curing diseases that affect humans. The author is happily married and is surviving with a wife and two children

www.ingramcontent.com/pod-product-compliance
Lightning Source LLC
Chambersburg PA
CBHW051430250726

48656CB00020B/1342